THE RELAXING RETIREMENT FORMULA

THE
RELAXING
RETIREMENT
FORMULA

For the Confidence to Liberate What You've Saved
and Start Living the Life You've Earned

JACK PHELPS

RELAXING RETIREMENT PUBLISHING

THE RELAXING RETIREMENT FORMULA
*For the Confidence to Liberate What You've Saved
and Start Living the Life You've Earned*

ISBN   978-1-5445-0398-1 *Hardcover*
          978-1-5445-0356-1 *Paperback*
          978-1-5445-0357-8 *Ebook*

CONTENTS

DISCLOSURE

The couples presented throughout this book are based upon a composite of real member stories, each of which had a particular set of goals and objectives, to illustrate various principles and strategies. The strategies described in these stories may differ from strategies implemented with other members, and the results achieved may not be similar, as every member's goals and objectives are unique.

The views expressed represent the opinions of Jack Phelps, founder and president of The Relaxing Retirement Coach, Inc. and are subject to change. These views are not intended as a forecast, a guarantee of future results, investment recommendation, or an offer to buy or sell any securities. The information provided should not be construed as investment advice or to provide any investment, tax, financial, or legal advice or service to any individual person. Addition information, including management fees and expenses, is provided on The Relaxing Retirement Coach, Inc.'s Form ADV Part 2, which is available upon request.

INTRODUCTION

In 1989 the passing comment of an older gentle-man changed the course of my professional life and launched a crusade that occupied my next twenty-nine years. He and I were casually discussing a new savings discount that allowed parents to prepay all four years of college tuition. His kids had already graduated, he said, or he would have jumped at the chance.

It hit me like a lightning bolt. I thought he was nuts. Like this man, my father had been a high school teacher, but my parents didn't even take a vacation for twenty-six years. Why did this guy believe he could have prepaid four years of college? How was he so confident when my parents worked hard but always worried about money?

Working to answer those questions, my research revealed that after a forty-year career, only a tiny percentage of Americans successfully retire independently to a same or improved standard of living. This struck me as incredibly sad. What made that tiny percentage so fortunate?

My first thought was the obvious one: they simply had more money. But that wasn't the case. In the twenty-nine years I've worked to develop The Relaxing Retirement Formula, I've met with very affluent men and women who faced every morning with enormous anxiety and lived like they might run out of money that night.

I immersed myself in studying this tiny percentage of successful retirees—their mindsets, systems, and practices. After extensive research, I identified the key difference between those who retire successfully to exciting, fulfilling lives and those who don't. The difference is financial confidence.

Where Confidence Falters

One of the biggest emotional, social, and financial challenges you'll ever face is the transition from working hard and saving prudently to no longer getting a paycheck. Even if you've done a great job building up substantial retirement savings, how can you be certain you have enough to live the life you want?

In phase two of your financial life, you'll no longer depend on income from your employment. Many of the old rules by which you built up a comfortable nest egg no longer pertain. The pension plans of your parents' generation are gone, and a financial mistake at this stage could be much more costly. Deep down, you're not 100 percent convinced that you have enough. After decades of working hard and saving well, flipping the switch from saving what you've earned to spending what you've saved simply feels weird.

Many couples facing this strange inflection point and uncertain of the precise dollar amount they can afford to spend without worrying about running out work well past the point when they'd like to retire. Others, without a reliable system to make their money last, start pulling punches, modeling their behavior on retirees they know who are living on a fixed income. They responsibly managed their finances through flush years and lean in the employment-dependent first phase of their lives, but now they recognize the terrain has changed. Within that new landscape, they lack the financial confidence to spend what they've earned and enjoy what they've saved for. Nobody, not even that small percentage I studied, is born with such confidence. They develop it.

Where Confidence Starts

Most people who have achieved a degree of mastery in their field recognize the value of expertise in every arena. Most successful individuals learned early in their lives how to benefit from the advice and guidance of others, and they actively seek out mentors and coaching. I grew up watching and playing football, so for me, the readiest example is Tom Brady, who at forty-one still has his own personal quarterback coach in addition to Bill Belichick. Top performers from Tiger Woods to Amazon's Jeff Bezos credit a coach or mentor with at least a portion of their success. As experts themselves, they recognize the need for an outside perspective and objective, professional advice.

It was a lesson I learned early. My dad coached high school football, and I grew up playing the game. I wasn't a star, but I was good enough to go to college on a football scholarship, where I played for some extraordinary coaches. My head coach, who went on to coach in the NFL for over twenty years, taught me something that became the cornerstone of my own coaching philosophy: it's the little things. It's wisdom I learned from him but proved to myself as I worked and studied to understand what separated that tiny percentage of Americans who retire successfully from the vast majority who do not.

As I analyzed how people find clarity and direction and achieve their goals, I realized there isn't a single big key to success. More often than not, it's the 5 or 10 percent you do and nobody else does that separates you from the rest and that delivers great results. It isn't talent or luck that puts you in the position everyone wants to be in. It's that you see both the big picture and the details. You catch the things others miss and attend to what they overlook.

A Relaxing Retirement

It was a lack of financial confidence that kept my parents from doing many of the things they had always wanted to do before it was too late (unfortunately, because my mother died young, this moment came quite early). It's been my mission since to help others who've worked hard and saved avoid the same regrets and to give to you what I couldn't give them: the confidence to liberate what you've saved and start living the life you've earned.

The Relaxing Retirement Formula provides the missing system, the checklists, and the exact numbers you need to flip that savings-to-spending switch with confidence and to start living exactly the way you want to. It will give you the following:

- The amount you can afford to spend each year without the fear of running out
- The one number that must guide all your investment decisions
- How to strategically and confidently position your Retirement Bucket of investments in all market conditions
- Four strategies to avoid paying more in taxes than you legally must
- Five tools you need to prepare for what you can't predict
- Four documents and a critical checklist you must have in place to ensure your loved ones are seamlessly cared for after you're gone

Just as a moderate diet and regular exercise dramatically increase your chances but can't guarantee a long and healthy life, no financial system can promise you an ideal future. There are, however, successful formulas built on highly probable odds in both health and finance. The Relaxing Retirement Formula isn't a guarantee. It's a time-tested system for playing the odds each step of the way and reaping the rewards statistics demonstrate.

If you're a decade away from retirement, this book isn't for you. It won't teach you how to save for college or pay for your kid's wedding. It's for couples who've already done all that. It's for people who were great at whatever they did to support themselves and to build up savings and who are now starting to wonder, "Do I have enough to retire if I want to? How much can we spend without worrying we'll run out? Can we afford to buy a second home to escape harsh winters? How do I position my money to last through all market conditions? What strategy should guide which accounts, and in what order should I withdraw money from my savings so we don't give it all away to the government in taxes? How should we protect our assets if I get sick and require extended healthcare? How can we avoid the delays and costs of probate and estate taxes and be certain everything we worked for goes to whom we wish? How the heck do I do all this on my own?"

The Relaxing Retirement Formula is for everyone who recognizes they're facing a significant inflection point. They're asking difficult questions and finding unsatisfying answers. The confidence with which they worked and saved all their lives is wavering.

They have no expertise in this new, second phase of their financial lives. They're anxious because they're smart. They're right; this transition is incredibly complex. They are standing at The Employment Dependency Threshold.

PART ONE

DISCOVERY

IS THIS YOU?

CHAPTER 1

DISCOVER WHERE YOU ARE

One of the first things Joe told me about Sally[1] was that she never complains. Sitting across from her in my conference room, I could easily believe it. Sally, attractive and energetic, told me that she and Joe met in college and that their last few years had felt a lot like their first. They both worked and had no kids at home anymore. Sally left her job as a teacher to stay home with their three boys but went back to teaching when the youngest started elementary school.

Joe and Sally did everything right. They maxed out their 401(k)s and 403(b)s, invested Joe's bonus each year instead of spending it, and funded 529s for their

---

1   Joe and Sally aren't real people. They're composites created for the purpose of illustration. Please see the Disclosure Statement that precedes the Introduction.

kids' college. All three graduated, two have since married, and their first grandchild just celebrated his first birthday.

At first, Joe told me, when Sally wasn't excited about starting the new school year, he'd thought it was because they'd had such a wonderful summer. All the kids had come to visit at the beach house they own on Cape Cod. But it was more than that. Sally had arranged for a sub to cover two weeks when the new grandbaby came, but she wasn't just wishing she could get away for longer. She wasn't sure she wanted to go back to teaching at all.

"It just isn't fun anymore," she told me. "It's gotten so political, and the new principal is unbearable. But I'm going to stick it out until I'm sixty-five to keep my health insurance. It's too expensive otherwise."

Joe hated to see her so resigned, and he'd begun feeling the same way. Many of the coworkers he'd started with were retiring, and the work culture had changed. His best friend retired two years ago and was having a blast, but Joe worried. He took a drubbing in the 2008 stock market crash, and although their investments recovered, he was keenly aware that a mistake now could mean they'd have to work even longer or even sell the beach house.

"I'm just not sure what we should do," Joe told me. "And I'm not sure why I'm not sure."

COACH'S CORNER

If you'd like to take The Retirement Confidence Assessment, download a copy at **TheRetirementCoach.com/formula**.

The Employment Dependency Threshold

The Employment Dependency Threshold is the term we developed to describe the set of concerns and questions that lead to wide-ranging anxiety and confusion when folks start to reflect on what they want out of life in their sixties and beyond. Major life transitions are usually fairly obvious. Most even come with their own rituals or parties. You go from unmarried to married, childless to parent, and even if you're not prepared for all the changes, you're at least prepared for change. The transition from the first to the second phase of your financial life isn't as widely recognized or discussed, but it's every bit as impactful.

In phase one of your financial life, you work and you save. You go to school, graduate, and go to work. You get married and start a family. You buy a house and save for college. You pay for weddings and family vacations. In phase one, people accumulate money in different ways and spend on different things, but they all share one thing in common: they all depend on the income from their work to support their lifestyle.

Phase two is not necessarily synonymous with retirement. Some people continue to work the same hours at the same job well into the second phase of their financial lives. The difference between the two phases isn't what you do. It's why you do it. In phase two, you do what you choose to, not what you have to. In the first phase, you depend on the income from your work to support you. In the second phase, you don't, so you have a great deal more freedom.

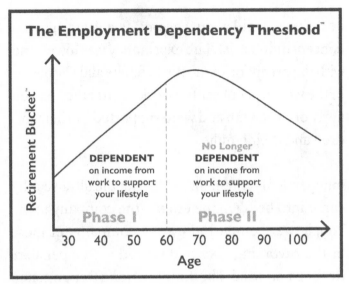

THE EMPLOYMENT DEPENDENCY THRESHOLD

Five Stumbling Blocks

Joe and Sally had a great deal to be proud of. They'd always spent less than they earned, and they'd done an admirable job of saving money. But they were still feeling worried and unsure of themselves, and with good reason. People in their early sixties approaching The Employment Dependency Threshold face five serious obstacles to a successful transition from relying on their income from work to spending what they've saved.

Retirement Is New

From a historical perspective, retirement is still in

its infancy. Until about seventy-five years ago, the concept didn't exist. Life expectancy was lower, and with the exception of the Rockefellers and Carnegies of the world, people either worked until they passed away or lived with and were supported by their children and their families.

Independent retirement for any but the ultrawealthy came into being in the era of "the company man." People were employed by one company for most of their working lives and retired with a pension. Retirees crossed The Employment Dependency Threshold with a contractual guarantee of a predetermined amount of money per month for the rest of their lives. Their finances didn't change drastically on its other side. It was almost like they were still drawing a paycheck. But things aren't so simple anymore.

In fact, the first obstacle Joe and Sally faced as they tried to determine whether they could retire was the increased complexity that came when private companies stopped offering pensions. Instead of being all in one place and under company management, as their parents' retirement savings were, Joe and Sally's were spread between multiple 401(k)s and IRA and non-IRA accounts. Joe had done a great job of managing the couple's finances for years, but he didn't have the same confidence his dad had when he retired. How could he? No one was guaranteeing Joe and Sally anything, and they were on their own to determine if they had enough saved and how to make it last.

Good Role Models Are Rare

Employers no longer manage their workers' retirement funds. They've offloaded that responsibility to the individual, so Joe and Sally can't look to the previous generation for examples. Beyond that, even with the explosion of information, education, and technology in the area of personal finance, only a very small percentage of people their age are financially independent.

A study from the Center of Retirement Research at Boston College in 2016 revealed that the combined balances in 401(k) plans per household were only $135,000.[2] More alarmingly, half of US households have none at all.[3] Their only source of income is Social Security.

---

2   "401(k)/IRA Holdings in 2016: An Update from The SCF," Center for Retirement Research, Boston College. https://crr.bc.edu/wp-content/uploads/2017/10/IB_17-18.pdf.

3   "401(k)/IRA Holdings in 2016."

It's unfortunate, but statistically speaking, it's unlikely that any given person a few years older than Joe and Sally would be someone they could use as a role model.

The Media Creates Anxiety

The financial media are all too happy to step into the void created by this lack of good role models, but they are not in the business of giving financial advice. The media makes their money selling advertising. The larger their audience, the more they make. Since investing, in and of itself, isn't very exciting, to build their numbers, they use skilled copywriters to convince viewers that the world's financial system is fragile and that markets could crash at a moment's notice. They condition us to believe that the only way we can protect ourselves is to tune in and watch. They don't sell us the news; they sell us the idea that we need to watch the news.

In October of 1987, the Dow Jones Industrial average fell 508 points in one day! At the time, that was a 22.6 percent drop—a crash by any measure. Today, 508 points represents just 2 percent, but the financial media still use points instead of percentages to alarm its audience. The media is heavily invested in having you believe your job is to keep a daily score on your investments, which is actually a terrible idea.

Everyone from Warren Buffett to Peter Lynch to Nobel-prize-winning laureates like Eugene Fama insists the last thing you should do is react to what's happening on a daily basis. The financial media use normal market volatility to condition people to think they have problems they don't. In fact, people who base decisions on imaginary dangers often end up with real problems. We'll come back to this in Chapter 5 when we talk about the bad results the average investor gets, but for now, it's enough to recognize the media as the third drain on Joe and Sally's confidence.

Politicians Point Fingers

Joe and Sally don't come from privileged backgrounds, and they didn't just get lucky. They built up their substantial savings slowly by working hard and spending moderately. I think they ought to wear out their arms patting each other on the back, but there's a subtle force at work that keeps them feeling uncertain instead of proud of their accomplishments.

Politicians know the same numbers I quoted above. To create a demand for their existence and to capture votes, they perpetuate the myth that markets are dangerously volatile and rigged by a few powerful insiders. Additionally, most of their constituency isn't like Joe and Sally, and "You should have been more disciplined" isn't a message that's ever gotten anyone elected. Instead, politicians cast people like Joe and Sally as part of the "lucky club" and promise to make things fair for all of those who aren't. Sally feels a little guilty about their prosperity. Joe, even though he intellectually knows otherwise, worries good luck did have something to do with it, and if it did, then bad luck might too someday.

Even Good Transitions Are Hard

The final factor working against Joe and Sally as they contemplate The Employment Dependency Threshold is the very thing that worked in their favor getting there: the power of habit. For years, they've been in the habit of working, earning income, supporting themselves, paying for their lives, and saving for the future.

"It just feels weird," Joe told me.

And of course, it does. How could it not? When you cross The Employment Dependency Threshold, you stop depending on your paycheck. Not only that, you must start spending what you've taken your entire life to save! It's going to feel weird. There's no other word for it. But all your years of discipline and saving, of building up money and investing it, are of no value to you now if you don't have the financial confidence to spend it.

> ## CONFIDENCE COMES FROM
>
> Understanding the unique difficulties and possibilities of standing where you are at The Employment Dependency Threshold.

Joe and Sally, it turns out, could have retired two years ago if they'd chosen to. Not only could they afford to keep their beach house, but they could afford to add more bedrooms for future grandchildren. The advice of friends and rules of thumb were never going to make them confident enough to start spending their savings without anxiety. Only concrete numbers and a disciplined system could give them that because The Employment Dependency Threshold is a daunting one to cross, especially if you're not sure what you want on the other side.

CHAPTER 2

———

DISCOVER WHAT YOU WANT

Kevin and Barbara came to see us looking for the same kind of clarity Joe and Sally had. In Part Two, we'll break down the process they went through, but for now, it's enough to say it's a bit like going to a very thorough new doctor. We took a complete history—financial rather than medical—and they revealed all their unique priorities to us. We put their numbers through an extensive diagnostic process over the next few weeks, and they returned to our office to get the results.

"Congratulations!" I told them. "You're in wonderful shape. Given everything you've shared, you can afford to retire tomorrow."

Can you guess what happened? Did trumpets sound and balloons fall from the ceiling? Did Kevin dance from the room and call his managing director to say he was finished? No. What happened?

Crickets.

Kevin and Barbara turned to each other, confused. Now that they knew they could retire, they weren't sure they wanted to. Kevin derives an enormous sense of accomplishment from his work, and Barbara would miss the friends she has through hers. They wondered if perhaps they didn't want to retire. They just wanted to know they could.

Of course, some of what Kevin and Barbara were feeling is tied to the inherent weirdness of the transition from doing what they've been doing for thirty and forty-two years respectively. Everything they knew was tied to their work—their friend groups, their sense of purpose, their pride in accomplishment. Work wasn't just something they did for money.

Much of their ambivalence was due to the lack of good role models we discussed in the previous chapter. Kevin and Barbara had seen a few friends retire and stop working. They'd watched the TV ads of gray-hairs in hammocks. They knew that wasn't what they wanted and wondered if maybe they just weren't ready to cross The Employment Dependency Threshold yet.

Conventional or Customized

Kevin and Barbara weren't interested in the conventional idea of retirement. They weren't conventional people. For one thing, they'd done a better job than most of putting money away. For another, they'd never aspired to what most people strive to afford.

As The Retirement Coach, my goal is not to get anyone to stop working. My goal is to get you situated so you never have to work—never have to do anything you don't want to—ever again. An ideal retirement for Kevin and Barbara looks nothing like Joe and Sally's. A truly relaxing retirement is one in which you do whatever you want with whomever you want where, when, and however you want with no anxiety about money. Your ideal retirement is customized to your ideals.

For some people, that means quitting work the next day, but a significant percentage of our members end up staying at their jobs because they love what they do. Many, with no financial necessity driving them, keep doing their work but stop going into the office every day. They work from home or from their second house down south during the winter.

Others go half time. Still others completely redefine their professional lives. They leave one business and launch a completely new one, sometimes in the same field, sometimes in an entirely different one. I've seen an operations officer become an entrepreneur and a software engineer go to work for a theater company. But they were both doing the same thing—exactly what they'd always wanted to.

Many of our members create a hybrid working retirement. They sit on boards or consult in their industries—doing so only on their own terms. They arrange their lives so they can go to warmer weather for six months a year and conduct their important meetings by telephone. They apply their business and leadership skills to charitable organizations, or they become mentors. Some hire a weekly landscaping service because they never want to do yard work again. Others mow their own grass into their eighties because they like the exercise. A relaxing retirement is one that frees you from chores and obligations that annoy you, not one that makes you give up any of the work you enjoy.

COACH'S CORNER

Retirement doesn't have to mean you stop working. It can mean anything you decide you want it to, and what you want can change over time. You're not locked into anything. You redefine what you do; you don't retire from doing it.

The Ideal Lifestyle

Drilling down to what "ideal" means to you requires that you set aside any fears and misconceptions you may have. Look at things you think are facts and question if they're really true. Call on your imagination to paint your perfect lifestyle. Since you're probably not going to live another ninety years, it's crucial to get started on this process now. Even as an exercise, it's a massive mindset shift to go from thinking about your responsibilities and constraints to imagining your dreams and freedoms. But that's what your savings can purchase. You prepaid then for choices now.

To help Kevin and Barbara start exploring their options, we asked them a slightly morbid question. It's one we often ask in meetings with new members. We have them imagine it's the day before their last day and ask them to reflect on any regrets they think they might have. In twenty-nine years of doing this, no one has ever told me their vision of the future includes more time doing menial work.

Try to come to this exercise without preconceived notions of what you think you can do. Resist basing your expectations on what your friends are or aren't able to afford. Come to it with a completely different mindset. Go in thinking you can have anything you want. Later, we'll put a price tag on it and let The Relaxing Retirement Formula determine whether or not you can afford it all. Because if you could, wouldn't you like to know?

CONFIDENCE COMES FROM

Having choices about how you'll live in the future.

Kevin and Barbara weren't sure they wanted to stop working, but they were very clear about a few things they were no longer willing to do, so I had them write up a list of nonnegotiables. They absolutely weren't ever going to miss any of their grandchildren's games in the future. For years, Sally and Joe had been inviting them to go on vacation together, but Kevin and Barbara had always said no. Their work schedules made it impossible.

"I'm getting old enough that I'm not willing to miss out on things anymore," Kevin told me. He wanted to do what mattered most to him, but he didn't want to have to take on a second career managing his money in order to do it.

In the end, Kevin and Barbara's customized Retirement Blueprint included soccer games, vacations, and funding 529s for both grandkids. Kevin switched from his salaried job to consulting work in the same industry. It leveraged his valuable expertise but allowed him to call his own shots.

Now Kevin and Barbara live in Florida six months of the year. He does his work over the phone, and she utilizes her experience and contacts for charitable work, helping to improve childhood literacy rates in both states. They're doing exactly what they want where, how, and when they want to without anxiety about money because they know the numbers they need to know to be confident.

Never and Forever

We do this exercise with every new member, but I invite you to try it out for yourself at home. Think about the things you're unwilling to miss any longer and everything you want to stop doing. List all the things you think you'd regret not having done. What do you never want to do again? What have you wanted to do forever but didn't think you could?

Create a picture of your ideal retirement that's as detailed, as exciting and inspiring as you can. Do this without putting any financial constraints on your imagination. Don't worry whether or not you can afford it. We'll work that out in Chapter 5.

CHAPTER 3

DISCOVER WHO CAN HELP

Tom and Christine were sixty and sixty-one and belonged to a private golf club, where they socialized with other couples they'd known for years. To Christine, it felt as if suddenly everyone was wondering about the same things. Should they start planning to retire soon? Could they? How does a decision like that get made? She ran her own business. No one was going to tell her it was time to go.

Tom was an engineer who valued expertise and appreciated a well-designed system. He was pretty sure he was ready to retire and entirely certain he didn't have the training to manage their transition across The Employment Dependency Threshold. Neither Tom nor Christine believed in gurus or magic bullets. They were pragmatic, thoughtful people, and they did very little without planning for it first. Tom did some initial research, but the more he learned, the more he felt out of his depth, and he wasn't too proud to admit it.

Four Filters

Tom and Christine didn't have the vocabulary you now do. They didn't know they were facing The Employment Dependency Threshold. But if you, like them, have ever turned to the internet for retirement advice and been frustrated by the unqualified and conflicting opinions, and by rules of thumb that aren't an exact fit for your situation, I'm sure you can empathize.

If you're like most of our members, you've learned to delegate over the years. Being an expert in your field, I imagine you understand the value of expertise. If, like Tom and Christine, you're ready to sit down and talk with someone, how do you decide whom to trust?

Imagine that your ideal retirement is an exciting new invention, maybe a revolutionary new software program. You know that well-financed companies would love to take your designs and run with them, so you're eager to patent your work. Would you try to do it yourself? You'd probably get a lawyer. Would you ask your neighbor, the real estate attorney, to write it up for you? Again, probably not. You'd know you need an experienced, vetted patent specialist.

There are over 300,000 professionals in the United States—investment advisers, brokers, insurance agents, and more—who make their living offering financial advice. To find those most likely to arm you with the confidence you need to cross The Employment Dependency Threshold into the second "do whatever whenever with whomever you want" phase of your life, you'll need to filter that crowd in the same deliberate way you'd look for a patent attorney to safeguard your exciting invention.

COACH'S CORNER

I've made a free consumer guide, "How to Protect Yourself: 13 Questions You Must Ask Your Retirement Advisor Before You Hire Them," available to readers of this book. Download a copy of the guide at **TheRetirementCoach.com/formula**.

The Fiduciary Filter

As a term of their licenses, doctors, lawyers, and accountants all have a fiduciary responsibility. They are all legally bound to act in their client's and patient's best interest at all times rather than in their own or that of the company they represent. You might assume the same is true of people peddling financial advice, but it isn't.

Approximately 90 percent of financial advisors are actually licensed brokers who represent large investment firms and insurance companies. They do not have a legal obligation to recommend what is in your best interest. Because brokers are only compensated when you purchase financial products (mutual funds, annuities, and insurance, etc.), they have an inherent conflict of interest in advising you.

Only Registered Investment Advisors (RIAs) have a fiduciary responsibility at all times to the clients they advise. RIAs are required to file a Form ADV Part 1 and 2 with the SEC every year, and they should be happy to show you their current one. If they aren't, they aren't a Registered Investment Advisor and have no legal obligation to act in your best interest. This simple screening question eliminates 90 percent of the field, leaving you with approximately 31,000 Registered Investment Advisors to sort through.

The question to ask: Are you a fiduciary?

The Brokerage Filter

Now that you have eliminated the 90 percent (approximately 278,000) of financial professionals with no fiduciary responsibility, the next filter separates those who work solely in an advisory capacity from those who are dually registered. As many as 26,000 of the 31,000 RIAs are also licensed stockbrokers and insurance agents. When they operate as an RIA, they must act in your best interest above their own, but in the same meeting, and without telling you, they can legally switch roles and operate as a licensed broker. Acting in that capacity, they can sell you a product on which they'll earn a commission without a legal obligation to place your interests first.

This arrangement does nothing to reduce or eliminate their conflict of interest. It does, however, hide it. It is legal and common for advisors presenting themselves as Registered Investment Advisors, with a fiduciary responsibility to their clients, to be dually registered. Even though their business cards may read "wealth manager" or "financial advisor," they aren't legally obligated to act in your best interest 100 percent of the time. Only 1.6 percent, around 5,000 of the more than 300,000 financial advice-giving professionals, are held legally accountable to do so.

The Specialization Filter

If you had a history of high blood pressure and both your father and your brother had passed away in their fifties from heart attacks, would you feel confident putting your health in the hands of the general practitioner who treats your whole family but also sees patients who have cardiac issues? I doubt it. Even if you would, the people who love you would probably insist that you see a top cardiac specialist.

The same level of caution should be taken when seeking advice about navigating the complexities you face at The Employment Dependency Threshold. Advice from a generalist is unlikely to give you the confidence you need. There is simply too much to know. You'll be better served by an advisor whose entire organization is dedicated to helping people who are in the same position you're in who are doing exactly what you're trying to do.

The question to ask: What is your specialty?

The System Filter

One benefit of specialization is experience. A surgeon who only operates on hearts will have performed more open-heart surgeries than one who hasn't specialized, but you still wouldn't want to be his first patient in a new hospital. Specialization allows for a depth of experience, but it doesn't guarantee it. Specialists with years of experience inevitably codify it as an effective and time-tested process.

A Registered Investment Advisor who specializes in helping people cross The Employment Dependency Threshold into a second phase of their financial lives defined by doing whatever they want wherever, whenever, and with whomever they want should have a highly evolved process in place. How else can you be confident you've covered everything and are staying on track?

This specialist's whole system should be shared with you in writing in advance and should provide a detailed explanation of where you are at present with a customized blueprint for how you'll get where you want to go.

Finally, it should also include regular check-ins no less than twice a year to review progress against goals and to adjust for any changes in the tax code, your life circumstances, and financial markets.

While most people would never endanger their rights to a groundbreaking invention or genius idea, too many try to do something very similar with their right to start living the life they saved for. You're an expert in whatever you did for a living, during which you exerted the discipline to aggressively save. Along the way, you didn't have the time or the guidance to develop the systems, structures, and expertise necessary to cross The Employment Dependency Threshold, liberate what you've saved, and start living the life you've earned.

Since 1989, when that retired schoolteacher's casual comment launched my investigation into what separated the tiny percentage of Americans who successfully retire and maintain or improve their standard of living from the rest who do not, I've been on a crusade. I was deeply troubled by the injustice of so many people who'd done such a good job of saving money being unable to enjoy what they'd worked so hard to earn. No one was talking to them about The Employment Dependency Threshold, but they still understood on some level that the way they'd been managing their finances was no longer adequate to where they were in life.

They were, quite naturally, feeling uncertain, and the media and their political leaders were feeding their anxiety. They deserved to be in the catbird seat but were sitting on the sidelines instead, worried and anxious.

CONFIDENCE COMES FROM

Having the expert advice of an experienced specialist who is legally obligated to act in your best interest 100 percent of the time.

If this is you—if you're approaching The Employment Dependency Threshold, if you're ready to start doing whatever you want wherever, whenever, and with whomever you want, and if you've done enough research to know who's best qualified to help, then there are three things you need right now.

PART TWO

KNOWLEDGE

WHAT YOU MUST
KNOW RIGHT NOW

CHAPTER 4

KNOW HOW MUCH IS ENOUGH

Bob was a "rule of thumb" guy. They'd served him well in his career as a medical sales director, and when he and his wife, Linda, came to see me, that's what he was expecting. In his mid-sixties and crackling with energy, he told me how much they had in investments and asked whether it was enough for them to retire.

I told him I didn't know yet. Sure, I knew all the common rules of thumb for this, but I also knew that confidence was what would determine whether he and Linda would experience the second phase of their financial lives with enthusiasm or with anxiety. Rules of thumb can be useful when you're searching for general guidelines, but they won't arm you with the supreme financial confidence you need at The Employment Dependency Threshold.

As an example, let's say that Bob and Linda had exactly the same amount saved as Kevin and Barbara did. They even had precisely the same amount of Social Security income. Using any of the rules of thumb you hear bandied around on financial talk shows, we might conclude that both couples have enough to retire. But they don't. If Bob and Linda retire now, there's a good chance they'll run out of money. Why?

Kevin and Barbara have paid off the mortgage on their house and don't have a second home. They seldom travel and only buy a new car every ten years—usually a Toyota. Bob and Linda still have $300,000 outstanding on a second mortgage they took out to pay for their kids' college tuitions and weddings. They own a condo in Florida and buy a new BMW every three years. Because Bob and Linda's desired lifestyle costs much more than Kevin and Barbara's, they must draw a significantly larger amount from their retirement savings each month to pay for it.

Fortunately, Bob and Linda had a great deal more built up in retirement savings than Kevin and Barbara did. Nonetheless, to develop the confidence they needed to start living the life they applied the discipline to save for, they had to go through a five-step process much more detailed than any rule of thumb. This process delivered an answer custom-tailored for Bob and Linda to these three questions:

- Do we have enough to retire now if we want to?
- How much can we afford to spend without the fear of running out?
- What's the real rate of return we must earn on our investments to make it work?

In this chapter, I'll go through the process Bob and Linda used step by step, and if you do the same with your own numbers, you'll be able to determine much the same about your own situation. Imagine how much more confident you'll be crossing The Employment Dependency Threshold with that degree of clarity!

The Retirement Bucket

Over the years, I've found it helps to visualize a bucket with inflows and outflows on which you'll depend once you no longer count on your employment for income. I'll explain how it works and refer to it going forward simply as your Retirement

Bucket. In the example above, we'd say Kevin and Barbara need to draw $6,000 per month from their Retirement Bucket in addition to their Social Security income. Bob and Linda will have to tap theirs for $11,000 per month because they have a higher level of Retirement Bucket Dependence due to their higher lifestyle cost. But until they knew the precise level of that dependence, the amount they had in savings was almost irrelevant to whether or not they could afford to retire.

The Retirement Bucket™

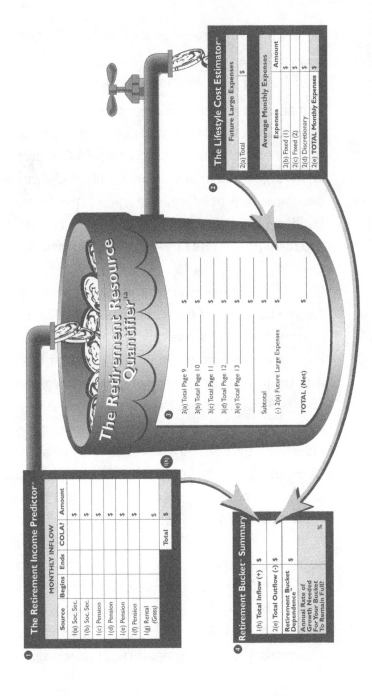

The Retirement Income Predictor™

Source	MONTHLY INFLOW			
	Begins	Ends	COLA?	Amount
1(a) Soc. Sec.				$
1(b) Soc. Sec.				$
1(c) Pension				$
1(d) Pension				$
1(e) Pension				$
1(f) Pension				$
1(g) Rental (Gross)				$
			Total	$

The Retirement Resource Quantifier™

3(a) Total Page 9	$
3(b) Total Page 10	$
3(c) Total Page 11	$
3(d) Total Page 12	$
3(e) Total Page 13	$
Subtotal	$
(-) 2(a) Future Large Expenses	$
TOTAL (Net)	$

The Lifestyle Cost Estimator™

Future Large Expenses	
2(a) Total	$

Average Monthly Expenses	
Expenses	Amount
2(b) Fixed (1)	$
2(c) Fixed (2)	$
2(d) Discretionary	$
2(e) TOTAL Monthly Expenses	$

Retirement Bucket™ Summary

1 (h) Total Inflow (+)	$
2(e) Total Outflow (-)	$
Retirement Bucket Dependence™	$
Annual Rate of Growth Needed For Your Bucket To Remain Full?	%

Determine Your Level of Retirement Bucket Dependence

Step 1: What Does Your Ideal Lifestyle Cost?

The first step to determine your level of Retirement Bucket Dependence is to get an accurate measure of how much your lifestyle costs. In Chapter 2, I encouraged you to envision your ideal life without the constraints of how you're going to pay for it, and I told you we'd put a price tag on it later. The tool we use to do that is The Lifestyle Cost Estimator.

It's useful to parse everything on which you spend money into one of two categories: fixed or discretionary. Fixed expenses are the boring things you have to do with your money on a regular basis to maintain and replenish your pantry, wardrobe, and garage. These are expenses you have in every typical year. You buy food and insurance, pay your taxes, and fuel your cars. These are all the "have tos." "Want tos," by contrast, are discretionary expenses, things like meals out, vacations, theater or sporting event tickets, and the like.

Beyond the fixed/discretionary divide, you also need to account for typical and atypical expenses. If you're going to buy a new car this year, you probably won't need to again in the next five. If your fiftieth wedding anniversary is coming up, though, you might earmark funds for a once-in-a-lifetime family vacation. Maybe you want to put money into a 529 college savings plan every year for your grandkids' education or make an annual contribution to a favorite charity.

Getting specific on your yearly typical and atypical fixed and discretionary expenses is clearly not very exciting, and part of my job as The Retirement Coach is to hold people's feet to the fire in getting a solid handle on this. The intention is not to create a budget or restrict your spending, and it's not because we care how much you pay for a haircut. It's because we want you to start doing whatever you want whenever you want. It's because we know that if you make only a cursory accounting of your expenses, you won't trust your own numbers, and you won't feel confident enough to join that tiny percentage of Americans able to spend what they've saved without anxiety.

You may not enjoy this exercise, but you will love the confidence of knowing that your answers as to whether you can retire and how much you can afford to spend are grounded in detailed, accurate data. The Lifestyle Cost Estimator has every expense item built into it because nagging "Did I miss something?" doubts aren't conducive to the confidence you need.

Step 2: What Is Your Predictable Retirement Income?

There are three income streams that flow into The Retirement Bucket automatically: Social Security, pension payouts, and rental property income. Obviously, not everybody has all of these, but there are two vital pieces of information you must know about any you do have: exactly how much is coming in from each source and whether any include an automatic cost of living adjustment (COLA). Social Security, for example, gives everyone an annual raise tied to the inflation rate, but most pensions do not.

Rental property income is a bit trickier to predict. You will, most likely, raise rents, but you will also need to account for the mortgage on the property, if you have one, as well as property taxes, insurance, and maintenance costs. The critical figure here is net rent—how much you bring in minus what you realistically expect to pay out. Our Retirement Income Predictor tool captures all these figures.

THE RETIREMENT BUCKET DEPENDENCE FORMULA

Subtract your predictable annual retirement income from your estimated annual lifestyle cost to determine your level of Retirement Bucket Dependence each year into the future.

Step 3: What's in Your Retirement Bucket?

This is typically the easiest part of our process. You inventory all your retirement savings vehicles and tally their value into a single number. Include everything you have in IRAs, 401(k)s, stocks, bonds, mutual funds, annuities, life insurance cash value, and bank accounts.

Step 4: What's the Timeline for Your Retirement Bucket?

An accurate timeline needs to reflect more than significant specific expenses you've anticipated in the future like a child's wedding, new cars, or an addition to your home. It also needs to figure in how long the money needs to last. How much you can spend each year is a function, in part, of how many years you'll be spending.

For a sixty-year-old couple, the average joint life expectancy is 31.8 years, or until they're ninety-two.[4] For a seventy-year-old couple, it's 22.6 years, which is 92.6 years old. If they're in better than average health, the numbers get even bigger. Statistically, the average eighty-five-year-old couple still has 11.1

---

4   Joint Life Expectancy is the age at which the surviving spouse passes away.

years for which to plan.[5] Bob and Linda had a retirement timeline of more than twenty-five years and a lot they were excited to get to!

Step 5: What's Your Plan to Combat Inflation?

With income, expenses, and duration factored in, inflation is the critical missing factor. The biggest risk you face is your income stream failing to keep pace with your inflation-driven rising lifestyle costs. Even at a modest 3 percent inflation, a sixty-two-year-old couple whose desired lifestyle costs $100,000 per year today will need $243,000 in the last year of their average joint life expectancy to support that same lifestyle. A seventy-two-year-old couple would still need $186,000 per year.

Here, our tool is historical precedent. As an example, in 1988 a first-class stamp cost twenty-two cents. Today, it's fifty-five. In thirty years, the price of a stamp, and of most other things, has increased 250 percent. It's not enough to have rigorously worked out the amount of money you have coming in this year if you want to feel confident that your Retirement Bucket will last. You have to account for

---

5   Male and female joint life expectancies based on Annuity 2000 Mortality Table. PG Calc Incorporated, *Annuity 2000 Mortality Table*, 2005, https://www.pgcalc. com/pdf/twolife.pdf.

inflation and its dangerous impact on your purchasing power. How do you ensure that the dollar in your pocket today isn't worth just fifty cents in the future? You invest it strategically.

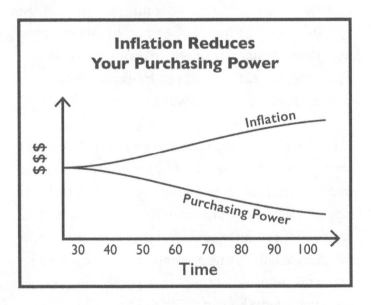

There are two ways to measure investment returns: the nominal and the real rate of return. The nominal rate of return is a flat measure of increase in value expressed as a percentage. The real rate of return is that number relative to the rate of inflation and its impact on your purchasing power. For that reason, when forecasting the longevity of your Retirement Bucket and evaluating how you should position your investments, the real investment rate of return you must earn is the figure to focus on.

A 7 percent nominal rate of return on your investments may sound appealing, but when you take inflation, as measured by the Consumer Price Index, into account, you may reach a different conclusion. In 2017 inflation measured a mild 2.1 percent. In 1980 it was a punitive 13.5 percent. In this example, with the nominal rate of return on an investment at 7 percent, the real rate of return was a positive 4.9 percent in 2017, but a negative 6.5 percent in 1980.

If you're counting on your Retirement Bucket of investments to offset the impact of inflation, you need to attend not to the nominal but to the real rate of return you must earn. As legendary investor Warren Buffett once said, "Investing is the transfer to others of purchasing power now with the reasoned expectation of receiving more purchasing power, after taxes have been paid, in the future."[6]

---

6   Warren Buffet, "Letter to Berkshire Hathaway Shareholders," 2012, www.
      berkshirehathaway.com/letters/2012ltr.pdf.

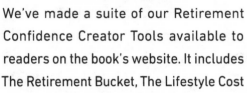

Determine the Real Rate of Return You Must Earn on Your Investments

We use a complex proprietary software to run Retirement Resource Forecasts based on the five steps above, but for our purposes, it's enough to understand that the real rate of return you must earn on your investments is correlated to your level of Retirement Bucket Dependence and to your retirement timeline. This crucial number provides you with two significant confidence-building benefits.

First, you will know whether the investment rate of return you must earn is historically achievable without needing to hit investment home runs every time you're at bat. Knowing that you only need to earn a conservative rate of return to make your Retirement Bucket last is an enormous confidence builder.

Knowing this rate also provides you with a target measurement against which to evaluate potential investments. On the other side of The Employment Dependency Threshold, investing without knowing this target rate is equivalent to having invasive surgery without first being thoroughly diagnosed. It's risky and dangerous.

We'll dive into investment strategy in the next chapter, but you can see how our approach differs from what you've probably been doing during the years in which you were saving for this time in your life. While your previous strategy clearly worked well, at this unique stage of your life, there are more obstacles to navigate, and the consequences of a mistake are much greater.

CONFIDENCE COMES FROM

Knowing your freedom to do whatever you want whenever and with whomever you want for the rest of your lives is predicated on a time-tested, custom-tailored, five-step process based on your unique priorities, timeline, income, and expenses. It's one that accounts for inflation and is designed specifically for life on the other side of The Employment Dependency Threshold.

Bob and Linda, you'll remember, had a higher level of Retirement Bucket Dependence than Kevin and Barbara, but they also had quite a lot put away. As a result, the real rate of return they needed to earn on their investments to fund all their priorities without the fear of running out was quite modest. We ran several Retirement Resource Forecasts, which showed them that, even earning a very conservative investment rate of return, not only could they maintain the lifestyle to which they were accustomed, they could also afford to spend another $39,000 every year for the rest of their lives. They could go on more vacations or open 529 college savings plans for their grandchildren. Or they could keep living as they had been and leave a sizable inheritance. No matter what they decided, they could know with confidence how much was enough for them to retire and how much they could afford to spend.

CHAPTER 5

KNOW HOW TO MAKE IT LAST

When we left Bob and Linda at the end of the last chapter, they were delighted knowing they had more than enough in their Retirement Bucket to support their ideal lifestyle. They were ready to start planning a vacation with both of their kids and all five of their grandchildren, but first, I had to ask Bob an important question.

When I was reviewing the investment statements he shared with me, I noticed they reflected a significant level of buying and selling last month. When I asked what triggered all the activity, Bob, not surprisingly, answered with a rule of thumb. Whenever it occurred to him to do so, he evaluated his portfolio and reallocated. He sold what had not performed well and bought more of what performed better. To the extent that this was a strategy at all, it was a strategy for ensuring he and Linda would run out of money.

Selling an investment that has recently performed poorly seems logical, but the appearance of logic is often misleading. In fact, what logic actually dictates is often counterintuitive. Over time, an average investor, like Bob, has historically earned 60 percent less than what markets have in the same period.[7] Fees account for some of that disparity; the lack of an evidence-based investment system is responsible for the rest.

In addition to earning a solid rate of return, investing on the other side of The Employment Dependency Threshold carries two more essential responsibilities. You must generate the inflation-fighting cash flow you need to support your lifestyle and gifting goals. You also need to keep your Retirement Bucket intact for the rest of your life. That's a tall task.

To be really confident that your money will last, you

---

7 According to "DALBAR's 23rd Annual Quantitative Analysis of Investor Behavior," during the same thirty-year period ending December 31, 2016, the average equity mutual fund investor earned 3.98 percent per year while the S&P 500 Index earned 10.16 percent per year. Ober, Terry. *DALBAR's 23rd Annual Quantitative Analysis of Investor Behavior*, DALBAR, December 2016

need a strategic investment system based on historical precedent and solid, evidence-based principles.

Five Facts History Teaches Us
Markets Work

Over the seventy-two years from 1945 to 2017, the value of the S&P 500 Index (a generally accepted proxy for broad stock market returns) grew 11.2 percent per year with dividends reinvested, which was 7.3 percent per year greater than the rate of inflation.[8]

Fact: Stock ownership has generated long-term inflation-fighting returns.

Markets Are Volatile

Over the same seventy-two years, stocks have experienced eighty-nine setbacks in which prices fell at least 5 percent. In three of those setbacks, prices dropped more than 40 percent.[9]

Fact: The market's long-term climb includes many falls.

---

8   DQYDJ *S&P 500 Return Calculator, with Dividend Reinvestment*, 2005, https://dqydj.com/sp-500-return-calculator.

9   Sam Stovall, *Stock Market Retreats and Recoveries*, American Association of Individual Investors, October 2017, www.aaii.com/journal/article/stock-market-retreats-and-recoveries.touch.

Markets Recover

In eighty-six of those eighty-nine corrections, market prices fully recovered to precorrection levels within fourteen months, with seventy-seven of those recoveries taking four months or fewer.[10]

Fact: All tumbles have been temporary, and most have also been brief.

Markets Couple Risk and Reward

The risk of an investment is measured by comparing its actual performance during a specific period of time to its expected long-term rate of return. Because a low-risk investment is unlikely to ever stray far from its expected return, only a willingness to tolerate greater short-term volatility can be rewarded by higher long-term returns. Any investment touted as offering high returns without downside risks is hiding something, usually fees.

Fact: There really is no such thing as a free lunch.

Markets Confound Navigation

Hollywood and the financial media cheerfully promote the romantic idea that investment success is

---

10 Stovall, "Stock Market Retreats and Recoveries."

achieved by an inspired expert ducking in and out of markets at just the right moment to buy before prices go up and sell instants before they fall. This narrative doesn't match reality. To equal the returns derived from continuously holding shares through all market cycles, such a navigator would have had to be precisely right on the moment to sell and buy 74 percent of the time. Only a few of the most famous market timers were right more than half. The very best was correct only 66 percent of the time.[11]

Fact: Continuously holding a diversified portfolio has produced better returns than even the savviest buying and selling for the overwhelming majority of investors.

Three Fact-Based Principles
Time Matters

Investing is a long-term solution to a long-term problem. In the short term, stock prices fluctuate erratically, but over time, their apparently random behavior makes sense. As Vanguard founder John Bogle has said, "Reversion to the mean is the iron rule of financial markets."[12]

---

11 William F. Sharpe, "Likely Gains from Market Timing," *Financial Analysists Journal* 31, no. 2 (March–April 1975): 60–69.

12 John C. Bogle, *The Little Book of Common Sense Investing: The Only Way to Guarantee Your Fair Share of Stock Market Returns.* John Wiley and Sons, 2007.

Principle: Having a workable strategy to deal with short-term volatility can help capture the higher expected returns stocks have historically earned.

Costs Matter

To make your Retirement Bucket last, you must pay careful attention to investment costs. Two percent in additional annual fees will cost a million-dollar investment earning 8 percent per year a staggering $2.3 million over twenty-five years.[13]

Principle: Be rigorous in your understanding of how much you're paying in investment costs.

Allocation Matters

In an effort to drum up business, Wall Street firms like to claim superior investment research that allows them to pick the best stocks at the most opportune time. This may or may not be true. It's almost certainly irrelevant. Strong academic research consistently demonstrates that superior selection had very little impact on results.[14]

---

13 One million dollars, compounded at 8 percent growth over twenty-five years, would grow to $6,341,181. The ending value after assessing 2 percent in additional annual fees would be reduced to $4,048,935

14 Bogleheads, "Fama and French Three-Factor Model," last edited May 12, 2018, www.bogleheads.org/wiki/Fama_and_French_three-factor_model.

According to Nobel Laureate Eugene Fama and Dartmouth professor Kenneth French, 95 percent of the historical returns generated by diversified stock portfolios were attributable to only three factors. Those three factors are broad exposure to stocks as a whole, exposure to smaller rather than larger companies, and exposure to companies with lower price-to-book ratios (value versus growth stocks).[15]

Principle: Allocation matters more than selection and timing.

Knowing What Not to Invest

With rules of thumb and reactionary buying and selling replaced by historical precedent and evidence-based principles, Bob and Linda are already in much better shape than they were, but they're not ready to start making decisions about their investments yet. Investing on the far side of The Employment Dependency Threshold requires a mental reframing. In this landscape, knowing what *not* to invest in stock-related holdings is worth as much as any hot tip on what to buy.

It may sound counterintuitive, but not investing 100 percent of your Retirement Bucket is one of

15 Bogleheads, "Fama and French."

the most important strategies for making sure your money lasts. The reasons are both practical and psychological.

As we discussed earlier, globally diversified stock portfolios have generated substantial long-term inflation-fighting returns. However, most Americans have not captured those returns primarily because they couldn't stomach the associated short-term volatility. On the other side of The Employment Dependency Threshold, this queasiness is even more pronounced for those now reliant on withdrawals from their Retirement Bucket to make up the difference between their lifestyle costs and their fixed retirement income sources.

For practical reasons, in order to provide for your anticipated withdrawals without the risk of being forced to sell when market prices are down, it's critical to have some portion of your Retirement Bucket held outside of stocks whose prices fluctuate dramatically in the short term. We recommend our members keep a minimum of five years' worth of their anticipated Retirement Bucket withdrawals in money market funds and other short-term fixed income instruments, and away from the volatility of their broadly diversified stock holdings.

Additionally, we recommend our members direct all the dividends they earn from their holdings into those short-term instruments instead of reinvesting them on the equity side of their Retirement Bucket mix. Doing so provides an even higher degree of liquidity to support their cash flow and typically extends their ability to meet their cash flow needs by an additional two years.

COACH'S CORNER

Keep a minimum of five years' worth of your anticipated Retirement Bucket withdrawals held outside of the short-term volatility of your stock holdings, and direct all dividends you earn to replenish your money market to support your cash flow needs.

From a psychological standpoint, knowing that you have all of your cash flow needs strategically planned for puts you in a position of strength. It provides you with the confidence to remain fully invested with the rest of your Retirement Bucket through normal and temporary market turbulence. Maintaining this discipline drastically increases your odds of capturing the inflation-fighting long-term expected returns of globally diversified stock portfolios. However, this can be a difficult shift psychologically.

Some of our members initially struggle with crossing the threshold into living on the money they've accumulated. They're so conditioned to accumulating rather than spending that they feel a need to squeeze out market returns from every dollar until the last possible moment to maximize their potential earnings. What was once an admirable habit can become a dangerous, even foolish, lack of strategy on the other side of The Employment Dependency Threshold.

CONFIDENCE COMES FROM

An investment strategy grounded in historical precedent, guided by evidence-based principles, and tailored to your specific needs and circumstances and to the unique conditions of life on the other side of The Employment Dependency Threshold.

To execute on this strategy, you have to get specific about your unique priorities and circumstances. There are four questions in addition to the real rate of return you must earn (which we discussed in the previous chapter) to which you must have precise answers based on your specific numbers. Because I can't know your specifics, we'll return to Bob and Linda.

Four Questions You Must Answer
How Much and When?

Bob and Linda have calculated their level of Retirement Bucket Dependence and know that, in addition to their fixed retirement income from Social Security and Bob's pension, they'll need to tap their bucket for $78,000 in their first year of retirement to maintain their desired lifestyle.

Because they've also worked through their retirement timeline, they know that in their second year, they'll need to withdraw $153,000 to pay for their annual expenses plus their daughter's wedding. The year after that, they're planning to buy a new car, so they'll want to withdraw $128,000 then. They're not anticipating any other big expenses after that, so for years four and five, they'll need $78,000 plus inflation.

Know the precise dollar amount of five years' worth of your anticipated Retirement Bucket withdrawals.

What's Where?

For tax reasons that we'll explore in detail in Chapter 6, the second specific you need to know is what percentage of your Retirement Bucket is in IRA versus non-IRA accounts. Bob and Linda need seventy-eight thousand post-tax dollars in their first year of retirement, so they'll have to withdraw more than that to cover the taxes. How much more will depend on how much they'll have to pay in taxes. We'll discuss strategies for reducing that figure in the next chapter, but knowing how to make your Retirement Bucket last depends on knowing what percentage of your savings is in IRAs since your tax burden will increase with that percentage.

Know exactly how much of your Retirement Bucket is held in IRA versus non-IRA accounts.

What's the Cost Basis on Each?

Bob and Linda inventoried all their savings as the third step of knowing how much is enough, and they've separated out their non-IRA accounts. Now they need to determine the cost basis of each of their non-IRA holdings. The numbers they log at this point will become the foundation for decisions down the road, but at this point, all they need to do is verify the price they initially paid for each of their non-IRA holdings.

Know the cost basis for each of your non-IRA holdings.

What's Your Required Minimum Distribution?

If you're under 70½ years old, the answer is simple—it's zero. The IRS doesn't require you to withdraw anything from your IRAs. Beyond that age, however, you must start withdrawing money from your IRA whether you need it or not because the penalty for not doing so is draconian. The IRS required minimum distribution you must take from your IRA is a function of your age and the value of the IRA at the end of the prior year, and unlike the cost basis for non-IRAs, it's a number you'll need to determine anew each year.

Know whether and how much you must withdraw from your IRAs and pay taxes on.

Four Steps You Must Take

Now that you've determined how much you need to position outside of stock market volatility, having a four-step strategy for the remainder is the final piece in knowing how to drastically increase your odds of making your Retirement Bucket last.

Determine

It's critically important to determine what percentage of your Retirement Bucket you should allocate toward the higher expected returns stocks have offered. Historically, the higher the percentage of your Retirement Bucket you can position in the long-term equity ownership of a globally diversified mix of stocks, the higher the probability of protecting your long-term purchasing power. Money markets, CDs, and bonds have barely kept pace with inflation, while shares in large companies have averaged returns of 7 percent above inflation since 1945.[16] Small-cap companies have earned even more.

Because you'll be counting on the cash flow generated from your Retirement Bucket to offset inflation's punitive impact on your purchasing power, it's smart to dedicate a sizable percentage of it to investments which have an opportunity to earn long-term returns significantly above that of inflation.

Diversify

Once you've determined what percentage of your Retirement Bucket to allocate to stock ownership, how do you decide in which companies you'll invest? It can be tempting to pick a single company—Amazon or Johnson & Johnson, for example—and many people do just that. Others commit to one idea

---

16 DQYDJ S&P 500 Return Calculator, with Dividend Reinvestment, 2005, https://dqydj.com/sp-500-return-calculator.

like solar power or to a single industry like healthcare or technology. Remember the dot-com era! I've seen people who only bought shares in companies located in their geographic region or exclusively overseas. I've seen still more who decide on a single asset class, like midcap growth, or settle on one investing strategy, like momentum.

But if you're going to invest your life savings in any one thing, that one thing needs to be a sure bet. And sure bets are easy to spot only in hindsight. On the day of purchase, shares in Apple and Polaroid may well have looked equally promising. It's impossible to predict with any degree of accuracy much greater than random chance which company, region, industry, or asset class is going to do Apple-well or Polaroid-poorly in any given year. Fifty-fifty odds are obviously not good enough. To improve them, you need to diversify broadly. On this side of The Employment Dependency Threshold, it's simply too risky to bet big on any one thing.

Delegate

You've decided to commit a strategic percentage of your Retirement Bucket to broad stock market exposure that is diverse in all the important metrics like company price, size, profitability, and region. Now you'll call on your grasp of historical precedent and evidence-based principles. You won't fall prey to the claims Wall Street investment firms make about their superior selection and timing. The same principle-guided strategy will also steer you clear of expensive, actively managed mutual funds since these have such terrible long-term track records. In the fifteen years ending in 2017, only 14 percent of actively managed funds out-performed their respective index.[17]

Index and asset class funds are a much more disciplined and cost-effective way to own a globally diversified portfolio, ideally one structured to pursue the higher expected returns historically found in the market, price, size, and profitability premiums. For this and other tax-related reasons we'll cover in the next chapter, the more of your Retirement Bucket you strategically position in low-cost index and asset class funds, the longer you're likely to make your money last.

Deescalate

Once you've executed on a post–Employment Dependency evidence-based strategy that's calibrated to your specific priorities and circumstances,

17 Dimensional Fund Advisors, *2018 Mutual Fund Landscape*, 2018, https://hub.dimensional.com/exLink.asp?30470202OA38T52I89531172, 6.

the final step you need to take to remain confident that your Retirement Bucket will last is to account for the natural escalation toward a more aggressive stance.

Shifts in market prices can change your strategically targeted allocation and increase the risk to which you're exposed. To counteract this tendency, we recommend a strict timetable of evaluation and rebalancing. This practice prompts you to do the necessary rebalancing regularly instead of reactively.

To see how this plays out in practice, we'll check in on Bob and Linda a year into an imaginary future. After accounting for their future cash flow needs, they allocated 70 percent of their Retirement Bucket to a strategic and globally diversified mix of stocks using low-cost index and asset class funds. Additionally, they moved 30 percent of their Retirement Bucket into money markets and the more stable short-term fixed income holdings we discussed previously.

In this hypothetical future, let's say stock market prices plunge sharply. Bob and Linda, of course, are fine. They can afford to calmly wait out the correction because 30 percent of their Retirement Bucket is held outside of the volatility of stocks and not subject to the precipitous drop in prices. But it's no longer

30 percent, is it? What had been 70 percent of their Retirement Bucket in stocks is now worth less, so their ratios have changed. Rather than 30 percent of their funds, their fixed income holdings might now represent 35 percent, so they need to rebalance to maintain their targeted exposure.

Moving money from their fixed income holdings into stocks at this juncture may well seem counterintuitive because it calls for them to move money *into* the depressed market. However, looking at this through the lens of a calm and rational investor who has followed each step in the formula thus far, this move means they're buying more shares of targeted stocks at reduced prices.

If we imagine a different alternate future in which stock prices soar, Bob and Linda would do the opposite. They would sell off part of their diversified stock positions to maintain their targeted equity exposure and would move the proceeds into the money market and fixed income side of their Retirement Bucket allocation to support future cash flow.

Bob and Linda have now replaced their reactionary and unplanned investment strategy with one grounded in historical precedent, guided by evidence-based principles, and tailored to their specific priorities, circumstances, and unique conditions of life on the other side of The Employment Dependency Threshold. They know precisely how much they'll need to withdraw, when to withdraw it, and how to strategically position their Retirement Bucket to pursue higher expected returns while still supporting their cash flow needs. They feel confident in their knowledge and are excited about their future, but there's still one threat they haven't addressed. They won't get to live the life they've saved for if they inadvertently give it all away in taxes.

CHAPTER 6

KNOW HOW NOT TO GIVE IT ALL AWAY IN TAXES

Bill and Rose like to joke that if Bill weren't clumsy, they wouldn't be in the fantastic position they are today. On his first date with Rose, Bill knocked her pasta plate onto her dress. The next day, he visited the neighborhood dry cleaners to prepay for Rose to drop the dress off and was disappointed to learn she'd have to make two trips—one each to bring the dress in and pick it up. He hated putting her through the inconvenience. Why, he wondered, couldn't the store deliver Rose's cleaned dress to her? He suggested such a service to the shop's owner and was hired on the spot. By the time he and Rose got married, Bill was running the store. He eventually bought out the previous owner and opened three more locations. Rose managed the accounts and brought the same efficiency and thrift to their personal finances. Now they were ready to turn the business over to their adult daughter and retire.

As with the other couples, once we'd developed a customized Retirement Blueprint, Bill and Rose were happily surprised and relieved to learn how well they would be able to live. They were confident in their ability to afford the ideal retirement lifestyle they had envisioned and were reassured by the evidence-based investment strategy we recommended. But it wasn't until we got into strategies to lower their taxes that Rose got really excited. She knew that every dollar they didn't spend on taxes was one that could go to dinners out with friends, to vacations they missed out on while managing their stores, and to their grandchildren's education.

Rose had always handled the business's and family's taxes, and it had been at her prompting that they had come to see us. She knew from experience that investment and tax planning must be done in tandem, and she was concerned about managing that intricate balancing act once they started to withdraw funds from their Retirement Bucket.

Politicians have created an enormously confusing tax code for us all to navigate, and Rose was keen to take every opportunity to reduce the amount of money she gave them. She showed me a quote she always carried in her wallet from federal appeals court judge Learned Hand: "anyone may arrange his affairs so that his taxes shall be as low as possible."[18] Or, in Bill's words, "It's not the government's money. It's ours."

I believe Rose and Bill are right. I think you have every right to legally reduce the amount of income tax you pay all the way down to zero if you can. And Rose is also right about the relationship between investments and taxes on the other side of The Employment Dependency Threshold. It is both highly complex and critically important. There are tax efficiencies you must take advantage of if you're going to make your money last.

People who make decisions about investments separately from the decisions they make about taxes pay a heavy price for doing so. I've separated the previous chapter on investing from this one on taxes for the sake of clarity, but I was only able to do so by tabling certain topics then and promising to come back to them later. The first of those, which we'll return to now, is the tax benefits of the low-cost index and asset class funds I recommended previously.

18 Helvering v. Gregory, 69F.2d 809,810 (2d Cir. 1934), aff'd, 293 U.S. 465 (1935)

What You Own

In the previous chapter, I recommended index and asset class funds as a more disciplined and cost-effective way to own a globally diversified portfolio. They're also highly tax efficient. If you've ever owned an actively managed mutual fund outside an IRA, you've probably already experienced having to pay taxes on capital gain distributions at the end of the year even if you haven't sold any shares. The value of the holdings could even have gone down, and you might still have owed taxes.

This frustrating lack of control over when you pay taxes is a function of the frequency with which managers of such funds trade. They buy and sell based on strategy, timing, shareholder redemption requests, managerial changes, and the phases of the moon for all we know. Index and asset class funds, by contrast, buy and hold a preset mix and trade only when the fund's mix no longer matches the index. This means that it's predominantly you, and not the fund's manager, who decides when you buy or sell and, thus, when you pay taxes.

Where You Own

Having discussed what to own, we now need to talk about where to hold what you own. In the same way it was helpful to imagine two different futures for Bob and Linda, it's useful to think about two different worlds, the IRA and the non-IRA world, in which Bill and Rose can hold what they own. Both fixed income funds (CDs, bonds, and money markets) and equity funds (stocks) can be held in either world. Where you position your savings within this complex geometry makes an enormous difference in how much you'll pay in taxes and, thus, how long your money lasts.

We recommend that you navigate based on what kind of income tax is assessed where. Because federal capital gains tax rates currently top out at 20 percent while ordinary income tax rates climb as high as 37 percent, it can be worth tens of thousands of dollars to position as much of your money as possible in the territory where capital gains rates rather than ordinary income rates apply.

The easiest way to see this in action is to look at several different kinds of investments and see how the earnings from each would be taxed in each world and how that should influence your asset location strategy.

Ordinary Income Tax Rates

- You pay ordinary income tax rates (maximum 37 percent) on interest you earn on bank CDs and money markets and on the interest and dividends you earn from bonds and bond funds held outside of an IRA or 401(k).
- All interest and dividends earned inside an IRA or 401(k) are sheltered from taxes. However, you pay ordinary income tax rates on the full amount you withdraw from an IRA and any gains you withdraw from an annuity.

Strategy: If you don't need to withdraw the interest from CDs or bonds, it's best to hold them inside of your IRA as long as possible. You pay no taxes now and keep accruing compound interest.

Capital Gains Tax Rates

- You pay capital gains tax rates (maximum 20 percent) on the realized profit from the sale of stocks, stock mutual funds, and real estate held outside of an IRA or 401(k) for more than one year. You also pay them on year-end capital gain distributions from mutual funds held outside of an IRA, even if you don't sell the fund.

- Capital gains on the sale of stock funds held inside an IRA or 401(k) are not subject to taxes after the sale. However, all funds later withdrawn from this world are subject to ordinary income tax rates (maximum 37 percent).

Strategy: Holding stocks and stock funds outside of an IRA allows you to benefit from the lower capital gains tax rate.

Selling a Stock Fund Purchased for $100,000 at $150,000

- If held outside of the IRA world, you pay capital gains tax rates (maximum 20 percent) on the $50,000 profit.
- If held inside of an IRA, you pay no taxes when you sell, but when you withdraw, you pay ordinary income tax rates (maximum 37 percent) on the same $50,000 profit.

Strategy: Holding equity investments outside an IRA allows you to benefit from the lower capital gains tax rate.

Selling a Stock Fund Purchased for $100,000 at $80,000

- If held outside of the IRA world, you can use your $20,000 loss to offset the same amount in other capital gains you've realized, reducing the taxes you'd be paying. If you earned no capital gains, you can offset $3,000 in ordinary income and carry the remaining $17,000 loss forward to cancel out future capital gains.
- Within an IRA, you derive no tax harvesting benefits from your realized $20,000 loss.

Strategy: Holding stock-related investments outside an IRA or an annuity allows you to potentially benefit even from a loss.

COACH'S CORNER

Whenever possible, position funds strategically to pay lower capital gains tax rates rather than higher ordinary income tax rates.

Where You Withdraw From
The Tax Reduction Decision Tree

Because they've done all the work in the previous chapters, Bill and Rose now know exactly how much they need to withdraw from their Retirement Bucket to support their ideal lifestyle. They know what they own, where they own it, and how much they paid for it. Now, when they're ready to begin withdrawing funds, they can determine which accounts they should tap, when, and in what order to reduce what they pay in taxes. They do this through a series of if-then forks on the Tax Reduction Decision Tree, which we'll walk through with them one branch at a time.

The First Fork: One or More Worlds?

One

If Bill and Rose's entire Retirement Bucket is inside the world of tax-deferred retirement accounts such as 401(k)s and IRAs, then the only variable they can control is time. A strategy sometimes referred to as "tax year straddling" may let them push some of one year's tax burden into the next year.

How It Works

If, near the end of the year, they temporarily tap and later pay off a home equity line of credit to buy time, or they withdraw only a portion of what they need and wait for the rest until 12:01 a.m. on January 1, they may be able to pay a lower tax rate by shifting the taxable income to next year, where the rest of their taxable income may be less. Otherwise, the first fork ends here.

More than One

If their Retirement Bucket is distributed between worlds, Bill and Rose can reduce their taxes by accessing funds held outside of IRAs, which are subject to capital gains tax rates, rather than those on which they would pay ordinary income tax rates. Additionally, if they have any realized capital losses either from this year or carried over from previous years, they can use those to offset gains, further reducing what they pay—sometimes to zero! To see how it works, we need to progress down the second fork.

The Second Fork: Over or Under 70½?
Under 70½

If Bill and Rose are not yet 70½, they are not legally required to withdraw funds from their IRAs. If possible, they should access funds exclusively outside that world, leaving their IRAs to continue growing tax-deferred since anything they withdraw from them would be subject to ordinary income tax rates as high as 37 percent.

How It Works

To keep things simple, let's imagine when Bill and Rose did the work of the previous chapters, they arrived at numbers identical to Bob and Linda's. They've subtracted their predictable retirement income from their lifestyle cost estimate and determined their level of Retirement Bucket Dependence. They know they need to free up $78,000 this year and next to cover their expenses, with an additional $75,000 in that second year when their youngest daughter gets married.

They inventoried all their savings as the third step of "Know How Much Is Enough." Additionally, in "Know How To Make It Last," they separated their savings housed in the tax-deferred world from the rest. They determined they had $1.5 million in 401(k)s and IRAs in the former and another $1 million in the latter split between the subworlds of fixed income and equity holdings. They know that they want to fund the entirety of the $78,000 they need over and above their Social Security and pensions from the $1 million they hold in that second world because that's where they'll pay capital gains tax rates, or none at all.

Their first step down the under-70½ fork is to determine how much that $1 million will have automatically generated for them. Let's say they'll earn $12,000 per year in dividends, so they'll need the other $66,000 to come from somewhere. But where?

To determine the most cost-effective answer to that question, Bill and Rose start with the unrealized gains and losses information they have in hand for all funds they hold outside of IRAs. If they sell any of their funds which have increased in value over their purchase price, they'll pay the lower capital gains tax rate on the profits. That's a great option to free up some of the $66,000 they need over and above what they've already positioned in money markets to support their cash flow.

Additionally, out of nostalgia, Bill has held on to some remaining shares in the first stock he bought, and these have lost value, as have two of the asset class funds Bill and Rose purchased last year. While initially this seems like a painful loss, if handled wisely, these funds can still be of significant value to Bill and Rose. Selling these out-of-favor positions would generate a capital loss, which the couple can use to offset the capital gains on which they'll have to pay taxes.

In the first year of their retirement, Bill and Rose sold off a targeted selection of shares, which balanced losses against gains and freed up the additional $66,000 they needed in a very tax-efficient manner.

Over 70½

If, at the second fork in the Tax Reduction Decision Tree, Bill and Rose were over 70½ years old, the path toward their goal of lowering their legally required taxes would look a little different. At this point, the rules of the first tax-deferred retirement savings world change.

The IRS allows you to defer the taxes on everything you contribute and hold in this world until you turn 70½, at which point it requires you to begin withdrawing a calculated amount each year. You'll pay the higher, ordinary income tax rate on the amount you withdraw, but if you don't take that required minimum distribution, you'll incur a 50 percent penalty in addition to the taxes you owe. Ouch!

Because they did the work of "Know How to Make It Last," Bill and Rose know their required minimum distribution will be $55,000 this year. They also know they need to free up $78,000. Sadly, this doesn't mean they'll need to fund only $23,000 from their non-tax-deferred retirement savings world.

Assuming their combined federal and state income tax rate on their IRA required minimum distribution is 29 percent, after taxes, the net amount of spendable money Bill and Rose have coming in from their $55,000 IRA distribution is about $39,000.

From here, the over-70½ fork proceeds along the same path that the under-70½ fork took. With their initial need for $78,000 halved by the $39,000 that's left of their IRA required minimum distribution after taxes, they take the same $12,000 that's coming in dividends, leaving them $27,000 to supply, using the same method of balancing capital losses and gains.

COACH'S CORNER

Where you withdraw funds from makes a big difference in the amount of taxes you pay and how long your money lasts. Take the time to strategically plan for tax-efficient withdrawals each year.

Bonus Branch: Charitable Donations

While most people are aware of the tax implications of charitable donations, our Tax Reduction Decision Tree offers a bonus branch that benefits both donor and recipient. To see how this works, we'll stick with Bill and Rose a little longer. They didn't go to college, but all three of their girls did. The girls went to the same school, which offered them generous scholarships and provided them with educations that continue to benefit them and, by extension, their parents. The entire family feels tremendous affection and gratitude toward the school, and Bill and Rose would like to give something back to the institution whose generosity made so much possible for their family. They've decided to donate $25,000 to the school in their children's names.

When we look at their Retirement Bucket to determine where the $25,000 will come from, we find two strategic opportunities. Before or after they turn 70½, in addition to making a donation using the traditional method of writing a check, Bill and Rose can donate $25,000 worth of appreciated shares of an index fund they hold outside of their IRAs. Assuming they paid $12,000 for the fund years ago, they could sell it, realizing a capital gain of $13,000 on which they would pay $3,250 in state and federal capital gains taxes. If they didn't make up that amount from somewhere else but simply donated the proceeds from the sale of their fund to the university, I'm sure the school would be delighted with the $21,750, and Bill and Rose would enjoy a tax savings of approximately $6,300.

But they could do better. If, instead of selling, they simply donated the index fund shares directly to the school, their tax savings would increase to $7,250, and they would pay no capital gains taxes at all on the transaction. Their children's alma mater could hold the fund, or it could sell it, and because non-profit organizations pay no capital gains taxes, the school would get the full $25,000 of benefit.

After they reach age 70½ and are subject to an IRA required minimum distribution, there is another tax-efficient charitable contribution path they can take that has become more advantageous with the passage of new tax laws. Similar to the last example, if Bill and Rose took their required minimum distributions from their IRAs and paid the taxes due, they could then make their $25,000 donation to the school and potentially be able to deduct the full $25,000 from their taxes if they itemized deductions on Schedule A.

To guarantee the tax-saving benefit of the $25,000 donation, this new alternative allows Bill and Rose to make a qualified charitable distribution directly from their IRA to the school. When they take advantage of this option, Bill and Rose don't pay income taxes on $25,000 of their $55,000 required minimum distribution.

The End of the Tree

Once you know what you own, where to own it, and have followed the Tax Reduction Decision Tree to determine from what accounts and in which order you should withdraw funds from your Retirement Bucket, you're almost ready to confidently start spending what you've saved and living the life you've earned. The final thing you need to consider is your targeted investment allocation. In reality, this consideration will be managed simultaneously as you progress through the decision tree, but for simplicity's sake, we've separated it out here.

While evaluating what to buy and sell in order to free up the funds necessary to support their lifestyle, Bill and Rose can see their carefully designed target allocation will now be out of balance. They aren't planning to sell a little bit of everything after all. They're making their decisions based on what will allow them to reduce their taxes. They'll need to make readjustments within the tax-deferred retirement savings world for the same reason. Inside this world, they can rebalance their holdings to bring them into alignment with their predetermined strategic mix without having to pay capital gains taxes when they buy and sell.

CONFIDENCE COMES FROM

Increasing the control you have over what you own, where you own it, and how much you pay in taxes.

You now understand the complexities of The Employment Dependency Threshold that you're facing, and you've gotten clear about what you want on the other side. You know how much is enough, how to make it last, and how to reduce what you pay in taxes. I hope you're feeling much more confident!

With the formulas, lists, and decision trees you now have, and with all your necessary information gathered and at your fingertips, you've made the discoveries and acquired the knowledge you need. It isn't all you need to start your relaxing retirement, however, because the unforeseeable may happen, and the inevitable will.

PART THREE

PREPARATION

WHAT YOU MUST HAVE
FOR THE FUTURE

CHAPTER 7

PREPARE FOR THE UNPREDICTABLE

When we left Bill and Rose at the end of the last chapter, they were ready to cross The Employment Dependency Threshold and embark on the ideal life they planned for themselves. They have, after all, done terrific offensively. But what about defense?

Imagine I let them go at this point.

Imagine they sell their business and retire. They liberate their Retirement Bucket and start enjoying their lives. One cloudy day, with everything going great, Bill is driving home from a round of golf and listening to the basketball game in which his kids' beloved alma mater is playing their hated rivals. The broadcast is interrupted briefly with some breaking news, and Bill wants to hear more from his trusted news station. He glances over to change the station, and in the moment his eyes are off the road, a skateboarder flies down a sloping driveway into the street. Bill brakes but hits the boy.

Of course, Bill and Rose feel terrible, and for hours, the only thing either of them can do is wait to hear how the young man is doing in surgery. They finally get some moderately good news. The skater is going to live. He'll even walk again after months of rehab, but he may never play sports again.

While there's nothing I can do to help with the emotional toll this will take on Bill and Rose, I can make sure they're prepared for this and other risks. They can take steps now to protect themselves from the financial fallout of such an accident and preserve what they've taken a lifetime to accumulate.

Four Big Risks

Very few of our members fit the stereotype of the retiree who's afraid of everything. Many of them, however, initially postponed retiring out of a media-fueled anxiety about the risks that might beset them. Bob and Linda were worried health insurance could bankrupt them. Kevin and Barbara had heard too many radio ads by elder care attorneys cautioning them not to let a nursing home take their life savings and their house if they ever got sick and needed long-term care. Joe and Sally had seen firsthand what the healthcare costs of a long illness could do to a couple's savings.

There are a lot of vague warnings and dire predictions in the air, but in reality, protecting yourself from the unforeseeable on the other side of The Employment Dependency Threshold is fairly straightforward. In addition to keeping up with your property insurance, there are four different types of risk—liability, death, long-term illness, and healthcare costs—to assess using three risk-management questions.

Of course, no one can avoid all risks completely, nor can you insure yourself against every potential loss without becoming "insurance poor" as Bob and Linda fear. Insurance can be expensive, as it should be. Rational assessment is critical. You need to objectively evaluate and then manage risk. Consider how likely any given risk is and decide how much of that risk you are willing to absorb.

Liability

Of course, I didn't let Rose and Bill sail off with only

an offensive strategy in place. They also needed a great defense. They already had quality automobile insurance with very high limits, but knowing that damages could (and in this case, did) exceed those limits, they also had an umbrella liability policy in place.

Liability insurance protects you from the financial fallout of accidentally doing something that hurts someone else. Very few people carry it, but it's not terribly expensive and is well worth it for the peace of mind it provides. Bill and Rose came to the smart decision to purchase umbrella liability insurance by asking the three risk-management questions we'll use to objectively evaluate the four kinds of risk:

- Without insurance, what is the potential financial loss?
- What's the probability that I'll incur such a loss?
- Am I willing to risk absorbing this entire loss myself?

Bill and Rose made the following assessment: the potential financial loss of having the kind of accident we envisioned for them could be catastrophic. They didn't think it was very likely (no one ever does), but they decided they simply weren't willing to risk having to shoulder the entirety of such a heavy loss.

Instead, they would pass on some or all that risk to an insurance company.

> **Preparation:** Purchase an umbrella liability insurance policy.

Death

Death, of course, is less risk than inevitability. Life insurance isn't designed to protect you from it but to provide some support for the people who depend on your paycheck if you're no longer around to earn it. Can you spot the issue here?

It's a paradox of life insurance that people tend to resist purchasing it when they need it most—when they have young children, a mortgage, and a spouse who either stays home with the kids or works part-time—but once they have it, they're very reluctant to let it go, even if they no longer need it. It can be difficult to think unemotionally about life insurance, so let's step through the three assessment questions.

Without Insurance, What Is the Potential Financial Loss?

If you've followed The Relaxing Retirement Formula up to this point, you've already determined that you and your spouse can live comfortably, enjoying the lifestyle you want and meeting your expenses by strategically managing your Retirement Bucket without depending on income earned from work anymore. If life insurance is designed to replace your paycheck, and you no longer need a paycheck, what is the potential financial loss of not having life insurance? None.

What's the Probability That I'll Incur Such a Loss?

Unless there's something pretty extraordinary about you, you probably aren't immortal. Statistically, depending on your age at present, your probability of dying in the next ten years is quite low, but death at some point in the future is still quite likely. But remember, life insurance doesn't offer any protection against that eventuality. The loss from which it does protect you is the loss of income from employment. What's the probability that you'll incur such a loss? Again, none.

Am I Willing to Risk Absorbing This Entire Loss Myself?

There are two circumstances in which the rational answer (and that's what we're striving for here to balance against the emotional response) might be that you aren't willing to take the nonrisk of absorbing this nonloss, but they're both quite rare.

- First, if you have elected the single life pension option, which pays out monthly as long as you live but ends at your death, life insurance can protect that pension income for your spouse.
- Second, if you strategically bought a life insurance policy as part of an irrevocable trust expressly to cover your estate taxes, it makes sense to continue paying the premiums on it.

Preparation: On the other side of The Employment Dependency Threshold, it's highly likely that your life insurance premium dollars can be better spent protecting yourself and your spouse from more likely and more impactful risks.

Healthcare Costs

Joe and Sally's biggest worry was that future healthcare costs could bankrupt them. This may be the fear I hear most frequently expressed, and it's certainly a reason some people continue to work jobs they no longer enjoy.

Although at first glance the numbers appear to support it, this anxiety is largely misplaced. Statistically, a sixty-five-year-old couple will pay $280,000 out of pocket over the course of their lifetimes for all healthcare-related costs.[19] But those costs are predictable and entirely manageable if planned for properly.

Additionally, once Joe and Sally turn sixty-five, they'll automatically be enrolled in Medicare, which covers most of the catastrophic healthcare costs they're so worried about. It will cover a sizable portion of their hospitalizations, doctor's visits, surgeries, and some medications. It doesn't, however, cover everything, so Joe and Sally do have a choice to make: should they buy a supplemental policy to cover what Medicare doesn't? Again, our three assessment questions will help them out.

Without Insurance, What Is the Potential Financial Loss?

As illustrated by the survey of out-of-pocket costs above, the gaps in Medicare can still add up.

---

19 "How to Plan for Rising Health Care Costs," *Fidelity Viewpoints*, April 18, 2018, www.fidelity.com/viewpoints/personal-finance/plan-for-rising-health-care-costs.

What's the Probability That I'll Incur Such a Loss?

It's quite likely that you will over the course of your lifetime.

Am I Willing to Risk Absorbing This Entire Loss Myself?

Given how cost-effective Medicare supplement policies are, there's very little reason not to pass along the risk that you'll incur costs for healthcare not covered by the program to an insurance company.

Two Important Considerations

Once they decide to buy Medicare supplement insurance, Joe and Sally must do two more things. They need to shop for a policy that matches their particular needs well, and they need to treat the premiums they'll pay for that policy like any other fixed expense.

There's a wide range of Medicare supplement policies available, and it's unusual for one to be empirically superior to another. Pick your policy based on your individual needs. Make certain it covers the doctors you like to see and your preferred local hospital. Some couples I've worked with take no prescription medications, while others take them by the fistful, and each tailors their policy accordingly.

Joe and Sally's Lifestyle Cost Estimator included line items for out-of-pocket medical expenses and for the premium they'll pay on the Medicare supplement policy. Make sure yours does, too!

Preparation: Budget and shop for a Medicare supplement insurance policy that's a good fit for your needs.

Long-Term Illness

So what about Kevin and Barbara's anxiety that they could lose everything if they ever needed to pay for a nursing home, assisted living facility, or care in their home? I feel for them. It's hard not to react emotionally to such messaging. We'll go through our three-step assessment process in just a moment, but before we do, it's worth taking a closer look at these grim warnings. Are they true? Who benefits from their propagation?

It is true that long-term healthcare is expensive. Costs vary by region and quality, but in the Boston area, where I live, for example, nursing home care runs in excess of $13,000 per month. Does that mean such facilities are scheming to take the homes and life savings of people like Barbara and Kevin? It does not. Nursing homes, assisted living facilities, and home healthcare providers are businesses. They provide a service for which they rightly should be compensated, just like any other business. However, how you choose to pay for such services is entirely up to you. They are costs that you can anticipate and for which you should plan.

Who benefits from stirring up this anxiety? On their business cards, they're elder care attorneys. They have the degree and belong to law firms, but they're most often also insurance agents who buy their ads with the profits they make selling insurance and annuities to the people they've frightened. Frightened people make reactionary decisions, and this is too important an issue to be made on anything other than thoughtful analysis of the fact-based answers to our three assessment questions.

COACH'S CORNER

Be on your guard for potential conflicts of interest if an elder care attorney makes recommendations on life insurance or annuities. Attorneys can also be insurance agents who make generous commissions for selling the annuities and insurance they recommend.

Without Insurance, What Is the Potential Financial Loss?

Statistically, people who move into a nursing home stay an average of two and a half years.[20] Using the $13,000 per month figure I quoted above, the average potential risk for each spouse is approximately $400,000. Importantly, while two and a half years is the average length of stay, 14 percent of people over sixty-five will need five or more years of such care.[21]

What's the Probability That I'll Incur Such a Loss?

Unsurprisingly, the probability of needing a nursing home, assisted living facility, or home health aide is a function of age. It increases over time, but 52 percent of those turning 65 will require some form of long-term care during their lifetimes.[22]

Am I Willing to Risk Absorbing This Entire Loss Myself?

Because we'd created a customized Retirement

---

20 Christine Benz, "75 Must Know Statistics About Long-Term Care: 2018 Edition," *Morningstar*, August 20, 2018, www.morningstar.com/articles/879494/75-mustknow-statistics-about-longterm-care-2018-ed.html.

21 Benz, "75 Must Know Statistics About Long-Term Care."

22 Benz, "75 Must Know Statistics About Long-Term Care."

Blueprint for Kevin and Barbara, we knew they could afford to withdraw $7,000 per month from their Retirement Bucket for their entire lives with regular cost-of-living raises. This amount, in addition to the income they earn from Social Security and Kevin's pension, allowed them to enjoy their ideal lifestyle with complete confidence their money will last.

But what if Kevin got sick? Now, instead of $7,000 per month, they need $20,000. And if that need continues for the average of two and a half years, their Retirement Bucket is going to run dry much more quickly than anticipated.

Realizing how financially devastating this would be for Barbara, Kevin was unwilling to risk their absorbing the entire loss, so we discussed their other two options. They could purchase long-term care insurance or strategically attempt to have the government pay for it through the Medicaid program. In the next section of this chapter, we'll go through their decision process, but it's worth noting first that not everyone comes to the same conclusion. While the answers to the first two assessment questions are fairly objective, the third is decidedly not. Whether or not you need long-term care insurance is individual to your financial situation and personal to your risk tolerance.

Rose and Bill, for example, ran the same calculations Kevin and Barbara did and came to the opposite conclusion. They opted to accept 100 percent of the risk themselves, confident in their ability to deal with extenuating circumstances. For them, it was the right decision. It was grounded in their customized Retirement Blueprint and tailored to their personalities and priorities. They had more in their Retirement Bucket than they'd spend in their lifetimes, even living their ideal lifestyle and funding 529 college savings plans for all their grandkids. Rather than give up money every month to an insurance premium, they decided they'd take on the risk themselves since, for them, the biggest downside was that, if they ever needed long-term care, they'd have a bit less to leave behind.

> **Preparation:** For most people, long-term care insurance is a valuable safeguard to protect the healthier spouse's lifestyle and to mitigate the potentially huge financial impact of the moderately likely event that one of them gets sick and needs care in their home, in a nursing home, or in an assisted living facility.

Long-Term Care Options

Kevin has a family history of heart disease, and he

vividly remembers watching hundreds of thousands of dollars in medical costs walk out the door of a neighbor who suffered from advanced dementia. He doesn't want to subject Barbara or his kids to what that family went through, so he has two options: Medicaid and private insurance.

Medicaid

Unlike Medicare, in which all US citizens are automatically enrolled on their sixty-fifth birthdays, you must financially qualify for Medicaid. To do so, Kevin and Barbara would need to drastically reduce their control of the assets on which their custom Retirement Blueprint depends. They wouldn't have to give away 100 percent of their savings, but they would have to give up their control over how it's spent. To do this, they could place all their assets into Medicaid-qualified annuities, which would provide an income stream to pay for care but would require they permanently relinquish total control over all funds used to purchase the annuity.

The other alternative would be to place all funds into an irrevocable trust for their children or a third party of their choice to control. This option is permanent. Once you give up the control of your assets, you never get it back. Additionally, you only become eligible for Medicaid five years after you meet the financial criteria. And finally, if you rely on the government to pay for your medical care, you're at its mercy to determine what care you receive and where you receive it. In my twenty-nine and a half years as The Retirement Coach, I've never seen anyone choose this option.

Kevin and Barbara were no exception. They didn't want to take on 100 percent of the financial risk that one of them might need long-term care, but they had no intention of relinquishing control over everything they'd worked so hard to save. Knowing that any insurance agent they spoke with would be highly motivated to get them signed up and paying their premiums as quickly as possible since that's how such salespeople get paid, Kevin and Barbara resolved to evaluate their needs themselves first.

Long-Term Care Insurance

If they hadn't already done all the work to determine the precise amount they could afford to spend each month, they wouldn't have been able to properly evaluate their needs. They would likely have ended up being sold the maximum Cadillac of policies, or they would have been quoted the premium on such a policy, shied away from its exorbitant price tag, and ended up uninsured and nervous. But Kevin and Barbara had done their homework. They had their customized Retirement Blueprint in hand. They were well positioned to educate themselves about long-term care insurance.

Six Main Components

By understanding the five principle parts that make up long-term care insurance, you can better control the premiums you pay. We recommend thinking about each piece individually and then in combination.

Maximum Daily Benefit

This governs what your insurance will cover per day, and you can dial the cost of your premiums up or down by adjusting this figure. Do some research in your area on the cost of care and put some serious consideration into what kind of care you're most likely to need and want.

Benefit Period

Benefit period refers to the duration of care covered by the policy. Knowing the average stay is two and a half years, you can elect to cover a finite number of months or opt for a lifetime benefit. The longer the benefit period, the higher the premium.

Elimination Period

This is a significant component, and deciding on the right number here can substantively reduce what you pay in premiums. The elimination period is similar to the deductible on your car insurance. A high deductible means a lower premium, but it assumes that you'll cover minor dents or dings out of your own pocket. Likewise, consider how long you can afford to self-pay for long-term care before your insurance starts to pick up at least some portion of the tab.

Kevin and Barbara knew that Medicare covers the first one hundred days of long-term medical care in a nursing home or assisted living facility or at home. They felt confident they could cover another six to nine months on their own, but they worried about what a year or longer would do to their life savings. For them, setting an elimination period of one year lowered their premiums without exposing them to unacceptable financial risk.

Home Healthcare

I've found that most of our members would much prefer to stay out of a nursing home. If they're not so ill they need to be in the hospital, they'd rather stay in the comfortable surroundings of their own home. If you share this feeling, it's important to check any policy you consider to make certain it provides the same level of coverage for in-home healthcare as it does for care in a dedicated facility. The range here goes from 0 to 100 percent, so if you feel strongly about staying in your own home, this is an important component to include in the policy you choose.

Cost of Living Rider

A cost of living rider is insurance on your insurance. It protects you against inflation. Considering the $13,000 a month I quoted above, it's difficult to imagine how expensive the same level of care will be ten years into the future. You don't want to do the equivalent of showing up today with twenty-eight cents needing to mail a letter. As with the other components, there's a sliding scale of benefits and costs. Cost of living riders can be tied to simple or compound interest rates, and the cost of your premium will depend, in part, on which option you take.

Shared Care

The maximum daily benefit, benefit period, elimination period, and options for home healthcare and cost of living riders are the five primary components of long-term care insurance, but there's a special feature of some that's worth mentioning. Most policies are structured so that benefits are split between spouses with a cap on each. Once benefits are used up by one spouse, no more coverage exists. With a shared care policy, however, you can more cost-effectively tap into one spouse's unused benefits to provide more coverage for the other spouse.

Maintaining Perspective

It's all too easy to get caught up in the intricacies of different policies and the various sliding scales they incorporate. Kevin and Barbara navigated the complexities successfully because they consistently reminded each other that their goal was to pass off to an insurance company only those risks they could not afford to take on themselves. They kept their focus on the large, long-term risk of care over an extended period of time, secure that their Medicare and supplementary insurance would take care of their other needs.

Additional Preparation

With the four big risks of liability, death, healthcare, and long-term care all adequately addressed, there's one more quick, free strategy our friends can use to prepare for the unexpected. In the interest of helping you do the same, we'll briefly imagine another catastrophe for one of them.

Let's say Linda and Bob finally get to take their dream vacation with all their kids and grandkids. They have a wonderful time, and even the youngest now has memories that will last a lifetime of the entire clan gathered at an outdoor table dipping bread in olive oil. Linda and Bob feel proud as they head home, if a little tired as they turn the corner onto their street. They're ready for a shower, some quiet, and sleep. They pull into the garage and know right away something is wrong. The windows of their second car have been smashed, the stand-up freezer is standing open, and there's an obscene cartoon spray-painted on the door into the house.

Inside, all their electronics are gone. Linda's closet has been emptied and the clothes used for fuel in the upstairs fireplace. Downstairs, their books have served the same purpose. The police suspect a group of drifters lived in the house for the better part of a week and stole everything they could carry when they left. But their homeowner's insurance will reimburse them, right? It can't replace the sentimental value of the photo albums and family china, of course, but yes, insurance will pay for everything— everything Linda and Bob can remember and list along with the date of purchase and current value.

Luckily, they'd followed our recommendation to spend a little time doing an inventory. They set out all their most valuable possessions—their wedding china, Bob's collection of cameras, Linda's jewelry and handbags, and her mother's vintage Joy perfume bottle—on the dining room table, and Bob filmed it. He then walked through every room in the house as Linda opened drawers and closets so he could film their contents. After that, he circled the exterior, getting the cars in the garage, the landscaping, and the outdoor cooking area.

Because the house hadn't burned to the ground, they still had receipts for their TVs and laptops, but they would have been unlikely to recover more than 30 percent of what they were due had they not had the video Bob made and saved on his hard drive and backed up on Dropbox. It jogged their memories, and it corroborated them.

CONFIDENCE COMES FROM

Knowing you're well prepared, even for the things no one can predict. You've rigorously evaluated your risks, logically and with strong assessment tools, and you've protected yourself against the most likely and devastating.

Even doing whatever you want whenever and with whomever you want, it's going to be difficult to enjoy yourself if you're constantly worried about what will happen if something unexpected befalls you or your spouse. In the face of alarmist advertising and genuinely frightening possibilities, The Relaxing Retirement Formula includes a disciplined and unemotional analysis of risks and a process for rationally addressing them. This empowers you to avoid buying what you don't need and to put protections in place where you need them most. Now that you've planned for the unexpected, you also need to prepare for the inevitable.

CHAPTER 8

PREPARE TO CARE FOR YOUR LOVED ONES AFTER YOU'RE GONE

Jane sat in our conference room between her two adult children, Susan and Michael. An obviously intelligent woman with a warm smile, Jane occasionally reached out to squeeze her son's knee or take her daughter's hand. Susan, in fact, had set up this meeting. Jane and her husband, Charlie, were friends of Bill and Rose, and Susan had gotten our number from Bill. He'd told Susan he thought we'd be able to help. I was just hoping we could.

Charlie had retired quite recently at sixty-six. Jane was sixty-four and planning to work one more year. A committed do-it-yourself guy, Charlie repainted their house himself every seven years, and he took care of their banking, filed their income taxes, handled their investments, and bought their insurance on his own. Jane described him as "old school," saying that he wasn't secretive but that he liked to hold his finances, his plans, and his information close to his vest. He never discussed such things with his kids, and he didn't talk much to Jane about them either. He was a guy who took care of things. Like Bill and Rose, he wasn't just the first in his family to send his kids to college; he was the first millionaire any of them had known. He was also the first to die.

Charlie had had a massive heart attack, and Jane, still reeling from the emotional impact of losing her husband of forty-four years, was in our office with her children when she'd rather be at home. She was there because she'd just discovered she had a list of serious problems she had to deal with immediately. Most pressingly, she thought Charlie had made funeral and cemetery arrangements, but she wasn't positive, and she didn't know where or with whom. She thought he'd probably written the information down at some point, but he was a bit of a pack rat, and she didn't even know where to begin looking.

Crucial Information Gaps

Not only did Jane not know what, if any, funeral arrangements were in place, she didn't know if they had a will. She was sure Charlie had once mentioned setting up a trust, but it was so long ago she couldn't remember any of the details. Neither she nor Susan and Michael knew if Charlie had ever used an attorney, financial advisor, or CPA. They all remembered him joking about his life insurance when the kids were young, but they had no idea whether it was still in effect or what company it was with.

Jane didn't have the key to their safe deposit box, the combination to their fireproof safe, or the password to Charlie's computer. She didn't know what bills were due or how to stay current and maintain their good credit. She didn't know which of their insurance premiums she should continue to pay and which to discontinue now that Charlie no longer needed coverage. She thought Charlie's pension might have a survivor benefit, but she didn't know how to find out. She didn't know where to draw funds from to pay for her expenses. She didn't know what investments they owned or what they were worth. Finally, because Charlie had left no instructions, she didn't even know where to start looking for answers.

Jane kept her poise, but I could see it fracturing under

the burden of so much uncertainty, which was only made worse by how helpless she felt. And how foolish. She wasn't just grieving, she was humiliated. Michael and Susan were heartbroken. They'd lost their dad, and they could do nothing for their mom. They were all looking at me, and I, dear reader, am looking at you.

If you, for some hypothetical reason, didn't wake tomorrow, would the people mourning your loss have that grief magnified by the kind of uncertainty and fear Charlie's wife and children were grappling with in our office? Would your loved ones have the answers Charlie's didn't? Probably not. In the twenty-nine and a half years I've been doing this work, I've yet to meet anyone who had all their critical information collected and organized in a spot where their survivors knew to find it. It will take you less than an hour to fix this, and it won't cost a cent.

My Request

Commit now to spending one hour of your next weekend to protect your family from this kind of unnecessary anguish. I know it's nobody's idea of fun to write out a set of instructions for your loved ones in the event of your death, but it may be the single most loving legacy you can leave them. It doesn't need to be carefully worded. It's not legally binding. It's simply "Here's whom to call," "Here's where those are," and "These are the passwords and combinations you'll need." Make a simple list of what they'll most need to know, show them the list, and tell them where they can find a copy. If you're so like Charlie that you find that too self-revealing, buy one red folder, put the list in it, and place the folder in the center of your file drawer with an appropriate label.

Jane and Charlie, by the way, aren't their real names, but these were real people, and this is a true story. I wasn't able to do as much as I would have liked to help Jane and her kids, but I made a commitment to do what I could to keep their story from playing out in other lives. Heading up this chapter with their story is part of how I'm keeping that promise. If you derive no other benefit from this book, I'd like to believe safeguarding your loved ones from a great deal of entirely avoidable suffering will suffice for us both.

> **Preparation:** Take an hour this weekend to write and share a list of the information your heirs will most need. Readers of this book may download a free "What to Do When I'm No Longer Here Checklist" at **TheRetirementCoach.com/formula**.

Alice's Story

Alice had been the primary beneficiary on her husband Peter's IRA, with their two children as contingent beneficiaries in equal shares. Luckily, when he retired, Peter had rolled over his 401(k) and pension plan into that IRA. Because IRAs allow for the tax-free transfer of funds from a deceased spouse to the surviving one, Alice had been able to move the money from Peter's IRA into her own. But when she passed away just two years later, her children lost over 40 percent of what remained of their parents' collective IRA savings to taxes.

Sadly, Alice's children aren't unusual. At least once a year, I hear a similar story. But this grim scenario is completely avoidable.

After her death, Alice's children called the institution where their mother's IRA was held to find out what their options were. They were mailed an IRA distribution request form, which they signed and returned with a certified death certificate. A week later, they had a check for the balance of the IRA minus over $922,000 in federal and state income taxes.

The kids' only comfort was that Peter and Alice weren't there to see how little of the money they'd worked so hard to earn and consciously save made it to their kids. Peter would have been devastated to see so much of it went not to the children and grandchildren he adored but to the government about which he'd never been much more than lukewarm.

Because income taxes on IRA distributions are assessed according to the beneficiary's income bracket, those who are doing well and presently need the money the least pay the most in taxes. Had either of Alice's adult children been struggling financially and in immediate need of the money, it might have been worth it to them to pay the taxes on at least some of the distribution. But they weren't, and it wasn't. They simply didn't know they had another option.

They could have retitled their portions to an Inherited IRA (also known as a "stretch IRA"), leaving their mother as the deceased owner with themselves as the beneficiaries, saving themselves a staggering amount of money in the short and long term.

COACH'S CORNER

Nonspouse beneficiaries can retitle an IRA to an Inherited IRA and continue tax-deferred growth for the rest of their lives. They must simply pay taxes on a smaller required minimum distribution each year instead of being taxed at their ordinary income tax rate on the entire amount all at once.

How It Works

Alice's children would have needed to retitle her IRA to an Inherited IRA by December 31 of the year after she passed away.[23] Going forward, they would be

---

23   This has to be done with an IRA custodian company who can and will do it, and not all of them will.

required to take a minimum distribution each year in much the same way Jane would have once she turned 70½. But because the children's life expectancies are much longer, their required distribution will be quite small, allowing the generous majority of their parents' saving to continue to grow tax-deferred.

> **Preparation:** Unless you're working with a seasoned retirement coach, photocopy this page now and put it with your will and What to Do When I'm No Longer Here Checklist to ensure your children will know they can retitle your IRA to avoid unnecessary taxes.

Thus far, preparing to care for your loved ones after you're gone has consisted of passing along two kinds of critical information—your written list of the names, locations, passwords, and recommendations and this page on Inherited IRAs. The final step is comprised of four documents that, once in place, will help ensure your assets pass on to your heirs as smoothly as possible. It will help minimize delays caused by probate and reduce the estate taxes they'll pay. The first three of these documents are straightforward and easy to set up; the fourth is as well, but it requires a bit more to explain why it's necessary.

Four Documents to Have in Place Now
A "Pour Over" Last Will and Testament

This assumes you already have in place the fourth document, a revocable living trust, which you should for reasons I'll cover shortly. A "pour over" last will and testament simply includes the instructions that all your assets not already titled to your living trust pour over into it.

A Durable Power of Attorney

If, at some point in the future, you are unable to make decisions for yourself, this document allows you to establish in advance the person you designate to act on your behalf.

A Healthcare Proxy

Sometimes called a living will, this document mandates who has your authority to make medical decisions for you if you're not able to make them yourself.

A Revocable Living Trust

This document isn't complex to set up, but you may encounter some resistance to putting it in place. Unfortunately, estate planning attorneys who draw up such documents have a potential conflict of interest that sometimes prompts them to advise against one for precisely the reason we recommend having one—it can allow your family to completely avoid probate. Probate, the often lengthy and consequently expensive process of validating a will in court, is a prime source of income for estate attorneys. A properly funded living trust can sidestep the process entirely—good news for your family but not necessarily for the attorney.

The case an estate attorney may make against establishing such a trust isn't dishonest. It's true as far as it goes. It's possible, even probable, that your heirs won't owe any estate taxes on your death. Federal estate and gift tax exclusions have increased rapidly such that, now, individuals can give up to $11.4 million and couples up to $22.8 million in gifts during their lifetimes and bequests upon death combined.[24] If your numbers fall below that, the attorney may not see a need for a revocable living trust. In fact, there may be no federal estate tax advantage to having one. However, three significant other advantages make a revocable living trust a better instrument than a

---

24   "What's New—Estate and Gift Tax," IRS, updated February 8, 2019, https://www.irs.gov/businesses/small-businesses-self-employed/whats-new-estate-and-gift-tax.

will for carrying out your wishes and caring for your loved ones after you're gone.

COACH'S CORNER

Because this trust is revocable, you can change your mind at any time. You keep all the same freedoms and control over your assets as you had before you titled them to your trust.

Control over Timing

A properly structured living trust allows you to specify when you want whom to get what in a way that a will does not. It gives you the power to delay passing on your assets to one or more of your beneficiaries while paying out immediately to others. You can stagger the delivery of funds over time or stipulate conditions on their distribution on a person-by-person basis, such as having funds available upon graduation from college.

Control over Circumstances

Setting up a living trust gives you the freedom to decide, in advance and with great specificity, what you want to have happen in every scenario: if one spouse is incapacitated and the other is not, if both are, if one is healthy and the other passes away, and in the event that beneficiaries divorce. A living trust allows you to spell out exactly what happens, who's in charge, who gets to make what decisions, and where your assets go. A will can't give you that level of control.

Control over Probate

We touched on this above, but having a revocable living trust represents such an advantage to you and your heirs over having only a last will and testament that it's worth understanding probate in a bit more depth. Validating a person's will before or after death requires that document be presented by an attorney to the court in the jurisdiction where that person lived. Once a judge declares it valid, notice is given to any potential debtors, and all the deceased person's assets are listed in the newspaper. Although it's time-consuming, expensive, and invasive, every will must be validated before it becomes a legal document on which anyone can act.

Living Probate

Living probate is a term used to describe the process of validating your will while you're still alive. It occurs if you're incapacitated and not expected to recover your faculties. Coma is a frequent trigger, but there can be others. Most people have strong feelings about the provisions they want in place for themselves under such circumstances, something a will can't cover. Because, unlike a will, a living trust goes into effect the day you sign it, it's an ideal vehicle to ensure your wishes are carried out.

Death Probate

Death probate is the process of validating the wishes you've spelled out in your will after you die. This can be a time-consuming, divisive, and costly process, but not until it's complete can your assets be distributed to your beneficiaries. A properly funded living trust can save your loved ones the heartache and delays of probate entirely. Your assets can pass directly to them without incurring unnecessary delays and lawyer's fees.

COACH'S CORNER

A properly funded living trust is an effective way to avoid probate.

Funding Your Trust

Setting up a revocable living trust is a terrific first step, but not until it's funded do its full range of advantages go into effect. Happily, this process isn't complicated or difficult. It simply involves retitling your assets to your trust now rather than having them all pour over after your death. This is a three-step process.

Apportion

Since you'll be establishing a trust for both yourself and your spouse, the first step is to determine which of your assets will be titled to whose trust.

Retitle

Change the title of ownership on each of your non-IRA assets from your name to the name of your trust. As an example, once you've done this for a bank account, your statement would read, "John Jones Trustee for the John Jones Revocable Trust" instead of just "John Jones."

Be certain to do this for all your non-IRA assets, leaving none out. Ask your estate planning attorney to spell out for you exactly how your beneficiary designations should read on your life insurance, IRAs, and annuities. Take care that all your beneficiary designations are updated at the same time.

Clarify

If you name your trust as your beneficiary, it may qualify for pass-through status, giving your beneficiaries the ability to take advantage of the Inherited IRA rules we discussed earlier in this chapter. Be sure to check this point with your estate planning attorney.

CONFIDENCE COMES FROM

Knowing your loved ones will be well-cared for after you're gone. They'll have the information they need, they won't lose up to 40 percent in taxes unnecessarily and all at once, and they won't have to endure the costly, time-consuming, and invasive experience of probate.

Charlie wasn't trying to hide anything from Jane or his kids, and Jane didn't mean to leave almost as much of their life savings to the government as she did to their children, but not intending to isn't the same as intending not to. Susan and Michael told me their parents took enormous pride in the work they did, the lives they led, and the savings they built.

For Charlie especially, part of that pride lay in knowing he wasn't doing it just for himself but for Jane and the kids. He saw himself as a great provider who tackled the work of managing their finances, insurance, savings, and planning seriously and single-handedly. He didn't want anyone else to have to worry about it. Sadly, this protective instinct exposed the people he loved most to a great deal of avoidable heartache he never anticipated. How could he have?

None of us knows how much time we have, and few of us have the expertise to protect ourselves and our loved ones from everything on our own. Charlie wouldn't have tried to represent himself if he'd ever had to go to trial. He didn't go in for do-it-yourself healthcare. He'd paid for private tutoring for Michael when he struggled in school and for one-on-one coaching when Susan got serious about ice skating.

But he carried a root-level anxiety about money throughout his life. It spurred his achievement, but it also kept him from enjoying the relaxing retirement he deserved. Think how different Jane's experience would have been if, when she unexpectedly lost her closest friend, her partner, and her sounding board, she'd been able to visit with someone she already knew, someone she and Charlie had been working with for years.

There was nothing Charlie could have done to keep his death from being a devastating loss for his wife and children, but if he'd had a customized Retirement Blueprint in place, their grief wouldn't have been compounded by fear. Pressing practical concerns don't have to pull focus from grieving family members' emotional needs if all the work is predone and plans are in place before they're needed. Loss is inevitable; a frantic scramble in its wake is not.

CHAPTER 9

PREPARE WITH CONFIDENCE

Over the course of the last eight chapters, we've identified multiple obstacles that can contribute to a lack of confidence as you consider crossing The Employment Dependency Threshold into the second phase of your financial life.

If you've read the chapters, experimented with the strategies, and followed up with the free bonus material on the book's website, you already know a lot more than you did. You now know where to be alert for potential conflicts of interest, and I hope you have a better understanding of your Retirement Bucket, how to determine how much is enough to retire, and how to make it last without giving it all away in taxes. You're already more prepared for the unexpected and to care for your loved ones after you're gone. I hope you're feeling more confident. But are you feeling confident enough for a truly relaxing retirement? Probably not.

The Retirement Blueprint

In the previous chapters, I've shared with you all the components that comprise The Relaxing Retirement Formula we use with our members. At this juncture, you're a bit like a couple I knew who wanted to build their dream house. They did all their research. They read *Architectural Digest* and cut out photos. They knew exactly the style and square footage they wanted. They even agreed about it! They bought a nice parcel of land and picked out everything from the brand of windows to the kitchen cabinet knobs. They could see their dream home vividly in their minds in much the same way I hope you can imagine what it will be like to start doing whatever you want, whenever you want, how, and with whomever you want. Like my house-building friends, what you need now is a blueprint.

You need a system that accounts not only for each individual piece of the formula as it's been laid out here chapter by chapter but one that also takes into consideration each component's interaction with every other piece, with the changing financial landscape, and with your needs and priorities as they alter over time. You need a comprehensive, personalized, and dynamic system, or you run the risk that the gorgeous spiral staircase you picked out will lead to nothing but the ceiling.

John and Diane

At sixty-two and sixty-three, John and Diane were eager to spend more time with their new granddaughter, and they wanted to start traveling while they were still young enough to tackle a safari. When John was offered an early retirement severance package after thirty-four years with the same company, he and Diane were thrilled. But they quickly started to feel nervous about making such a huge transition on their own and decided to work with an advisor from a well-known national company.

On their new broker's recommendation, John withdrew the balances in his 401(k) and pension fund and rolled everything over into an IRA at the advisor's firm. The broker recommended investments that were currently doing well, and John and Diane followed those recommendations. I'll bet you can already spot several errors they've made.

Unfortunately, their advisor never took the time to understand the ideal retirement lifestyle John and Diane had dreamed of. He had run no forecasts based on their priorities and their resources, and he hadn't calculated the real rate of return they needed to earn to support that lifestyle without running out of money. His investment recommendations were entirely untethered to any of John and Diane's goals. Instead, they were tied to his own goals of making commissions as quickly as possible and to those of his typical clients investing during the earlier stages of their lives and depending on their employment to support their lifestyle.

With the amount of money they'd accumulated in their Retirement Bucket, John and Diane needed to earn only a modest rate of return on their investments to keep pace with inflation and live exactly the way they wanted to. They didn't need to be aggressive with all their investments. But their advisor had over 96 percent of their life savings in individual stocks and stock mutual funds, gambling on one asset class of stocks with a long history of high levels of volatility. They did very well for two years before the value of their Retirement Bucket of investments fell over 63.5 percent, a rate far higher than broad equity market indexes experienced.

Additionally, they had made their investment and withdrawal decisions without considering the huge impact they had on their income taxes. They didn't have a plan for managing the significant risks of a lawsuit or long-term illness, or for passing on everything they'd worked so hard to accumulate without the time-consuming, expensive, and invasive experience of probate.

In the end, because their advisor didn't understand or care about the unique needs of his post–Employment Dependency clients, John and Diane were left with three choices. First, they could reallocate their remaining savings, being less aggressive than they had been but still exposing themselves to more risk than they would have needed to if they'd gotten better advice at the start. Second, they could make significant cutbacks in their lifestyle, or third, they could reenter the workforce to make up for their lost savings, something their health might prevent them from doing at some point.

No one wants to be a John and Diane, but their story is all too real. Worse, anxiety about having a similar experience keeps many more people from confidently spending what they've saved and living the life they've earned. Twenty-nine years ago, I set out to do something about that lack of financial confidence. In the time since, I've learned that there are two things without which no one can feel truly confident on the other side of The Employment Dependency Threshold. You must have a system and an ongoing strategy.

Systems and Strategies

What happened to John and Diane came about because they didn't have a system in place. Without one, it was too easy for them to fall prey to a slick salesman peddling the latest gimmicks. Without one, they didn't know how to avoid paying more in taxes than they had to. A Retirement Blueprint is a system for managing all the separate components of life on the other side of The Employment Dependency Threshold, for balancing each against the other, and for significantly increasing your odds that nothing gets missed.

A strategy is a plan for implementing and managing a system over time. Strategy allows you to customize your system to your unique needs and priorities and to adjust it when your circumstances change. If a blueprint is a system for building a house, a general contractor manages the strategy. When you're building your dream home, you need an expert to interpret the architect's drawing, sequence construction, and secure the necessary permits. The general contractor is your coach, responsible for your house-building strategy. Your dream house, your son's dream of playing college ball, and your family's dream vacation all require coaching. Your dream retirement is no different.

Retirement Coaching

Everyone needs a person to function as a sounding board. You need an expert you can turn to for advice, someone who's kept up on changes in the industry, the markets, and the tax code. More than anything else, you need support to withstand market pressures, to remind you of your customized long-term system and of historical principles, and to keep you from making emotional, reactive, bad decisions. An independent retirement coach brings perspective, expertise, and objectivity.

It's my hope that reading this book has given you a much broader understanding of all the components you need to include in your Retirement Blueprint, but sadly, I can only know you as a reader. From my position behind the page, I can't tailor my advice. I don't know your situation, your goals and ideals, or your anxieties or concerns. I can share our formula for a relaxing retirement with you, but I can't help you implement it. I can't customize it to your situation or adjust it as your unique circumstance or the world changes. No book can give you what you need to stay confident in all conditions. For that, you need a working relationship with a person. At The Employment Dependency Threshold, you need a coach.

John and Diane never fully recovered from the path the wrong advisor led them down. John took on a few consulting clients but found his memory wasn't as reliable as it had been. After two years, unwilling to turn in an inferior performance, he quit. They sold their vacation home and returned to some of the frugality that had allowed them to build up their nest egg in the first place. They were fine, although they didn't contribute as much to their grandchildren's education as they would have liked.

I never met John and Diane. They had been friends of Bob and Linda's and were, in fact, the reason that couple sought us out. When they told us the story, Bob said that even though John and Diane were never in danger of being a burden on their children, he wasn't sure they ever felt entirely safe. Their retirement was secure but not relaxing because they were never truly confident.

CONFIDENCE COMES FROM

Having a time-tested system tailored to your unique situation in a customized Retirement Blueprint managed strategically and supported by a seasoned retirement coach whom you know intimately and who is legally obligated to act in your best interest 100 percent of the time.

CONCLUSION

Each of the case studies in this book are composites of couples I've worked with for years whose names, numbers, and identifying circumstances have been changed, but I'll close with a personal story that happened not too long ago and exactly the way I'll tell it.

In a single two-week period, I learned that one of our members, a woman I'd worked with for years, had been diagnosed with aggressive pancreatic cancer and that another member's rapidly progressing Alzheimer's now required he not be left alone. I heard from yet another member that his wife, after five years in remission, was back in the hospital and soon to start a new round of chemotherapy. And finally, one of our newer members, who had only retired the last year, developed a degenerative nerve disease that had already cost him much of his eyesight.

I have close personal relationships with our members, and the loss of any is always an emotional blow, but the convergence of all this bad news in a short period felt like a wake-up call. We've all heard the advice not to wait for a crisis to plan for a crisis, and it would be great if it didn't so often require a major upset in life to motivate us to think and prioritize differently. This one propelled me into writing this book.

For me, the first such crisis struck when my mother got sick and passed away at fifty-seven when I was only twenty. The lesson I took from that personal tragedy was never to wait to enjoy the fruits of your work. Her loss prompted my exploration of why such a small percentage of affluent people get to enjoy relaxed and fulfilling retirements. While I would have preferred it didn't take losing my mother to learn that lesson, I've found real satisfaction in my crusade as The Relaxing Retirement Coach, helping others secure for themselves what my mother didn't get to enjoy.

If I've done my job in these pages, you now have a much clearer view of where you are here at The Employment Dependency Threshold. You've gained some insight into why this unique inflection point feels the way it does and into the higher stakes and exciting possibilities that come with it. You understand how to determine if you have enough to retire. We've talked through the way we forecast how much you can afford to spend without the anxiety of running out and how you can determine the real investment rate of return you must earn to make it work. You know the importance of reducing what you pay in taxes, and you have a decision tree to follow to help you do so strategically. You're better prepared for the unpredictable and to care for your loved ones after you're gone. You have the pieces. I hope you're closer to having the confidence to liberate what you've saved and start living the life you've earned.

If you haven't yet experimented with the free tools and resources I've made available on this book's website, I recommend taking advantage of them now. They're a great next step.

TheRetirementCoach.com/formula

ABOUT THE AUTHOR

JACK PHELPS left a career with a large financial services firm in order to offer independent advice in the best interests of his members rather than his employer. In the twenty-five years since, he's become an impassioned advocate and guide for people facing the complex transition from a lifetime of working hard and saving smartly to spending and enjoying what they've built. A college athlete, Jack knows the profound difference a great coach can make, and combines a coach's rigor and gift for explanation with years of education and hands-on experience in finance. Learn more about The Relaxing Retirement Coaching Program at: **TheRetirementCoach.com**.